PAST MASTERS OF THE

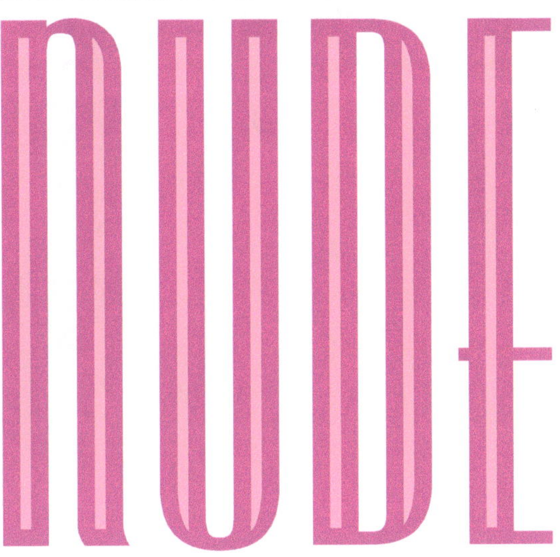

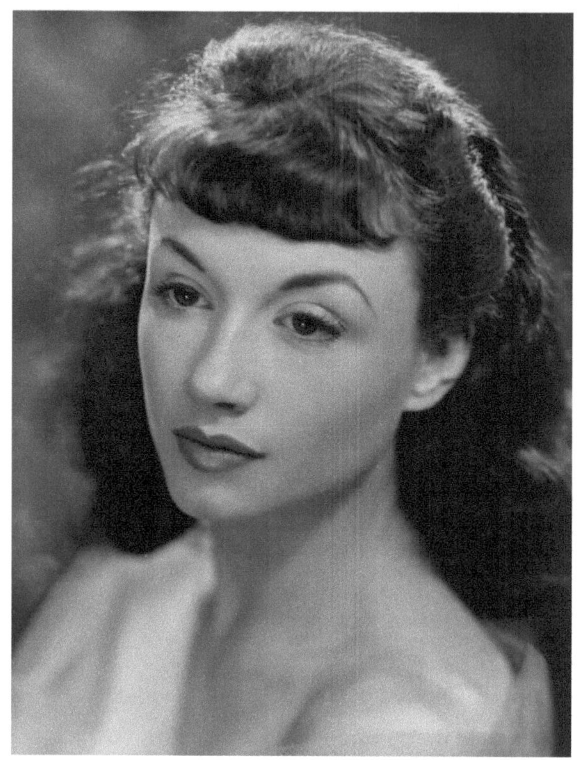

Dedicated to the memory of Pamela Green (1929–2010)

Published in 2020 by Wolfbait Books © 2020

www.wolfbait.co.uk

ISBN: 978-1-9162151-1-5

First published in 2005 by Kingsfield Publications
Second revised edition, 2013
© Jay W. King

PAST MASTERS OF THE

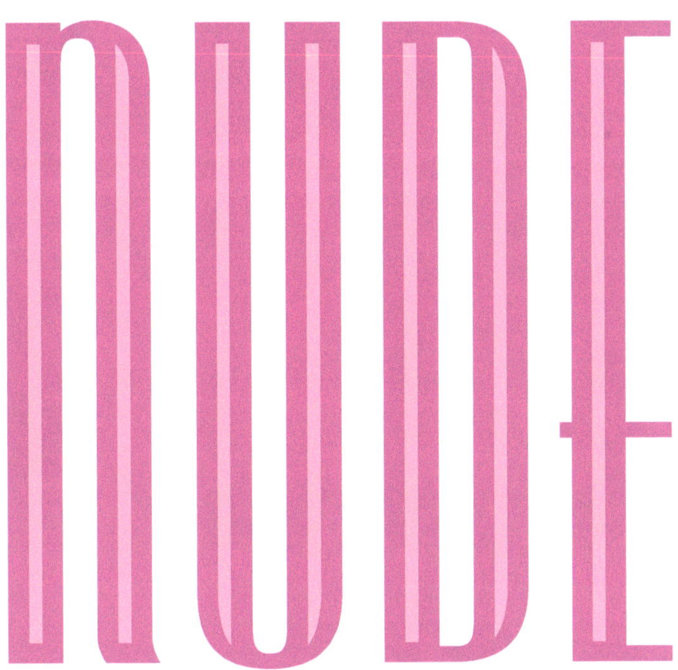

NUDE

An Illustrated Bibliography of Nude Photography Books
Published in England from 1896 to 1960

JAY W. KING

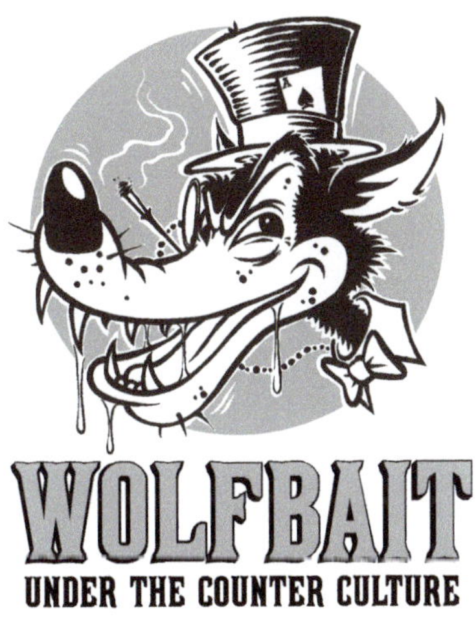

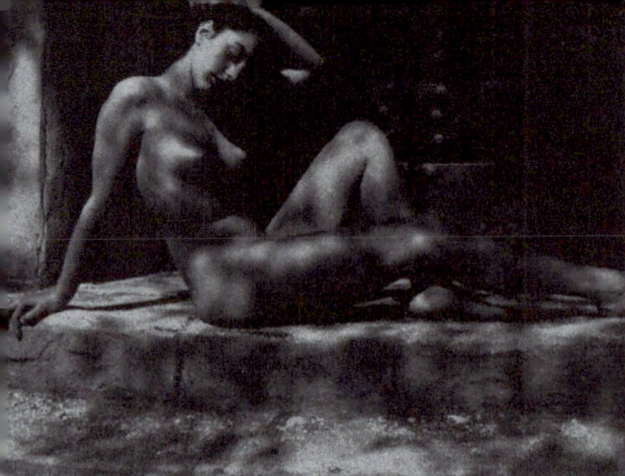

ALSO TWO FINE BOOKS BY A GREAT PHOTOGRAPHER

JOHN EVERARD

ARTIST'S MODEL 1,200 photographs *of the human figure and* **SECOND SITTING over 1,000** *photographs in full page studies and miniatures of the same pose from various angles.*

Never before have such fascinating and complete collections of nude studies been made available. The poses, domestic, fashion and artistic are invaluable to photographers and commercial artists and include child and male studies.

Both books 37s. post free

All books listed are available from

CAMERA STUDIES CLUB, 23 CHESHAM STREET, S.W.1.

Sculptor's Model

JOHN EVERARD

In his new book John Everard follows up the success of *Artist's Model* and *Second Sitting*. These earlier works were specifically designed to meet the needs of a vast potential audience of commercial artists and art students, and the fact that their combined sales now total nearly 50,000 copies is ample testimony that they supplied this demand.

This book is intended particularly to help the sculptor, and the poses chosen have the statuesque quality of that monumental art. It follows its predecessors closely in design. There is the same lay-out of one full-page study facing a number of photographs of the same pose taken from different angles. Once more the photographer has caught men, women and children not only in the studied shot but in the attitudes of their day-to-day activities.

If it is to the sculptor that this book will make its first appeal, other students of human anatomy will find it no less valuable as a work of reference. Enriched by those fine studies which make John Everard one of the leading photographers of the human figure, the volume contains over one thousand photographs of different models in a wide range of poses. It will be eagerly sought after by artists and sculptors who for one reason or another are unable to obtain the services of a suitable model; and by photographers, who will find particularly instructive the information which Mr. Everard supplies about his equipment and methods.

10¾″ × 8½″   200 pages   44s *(Post free)*

Obtainable from
THE CAMERA STUDIES CLUB
23 CHESHAM STREET
LONDON, S.W.1

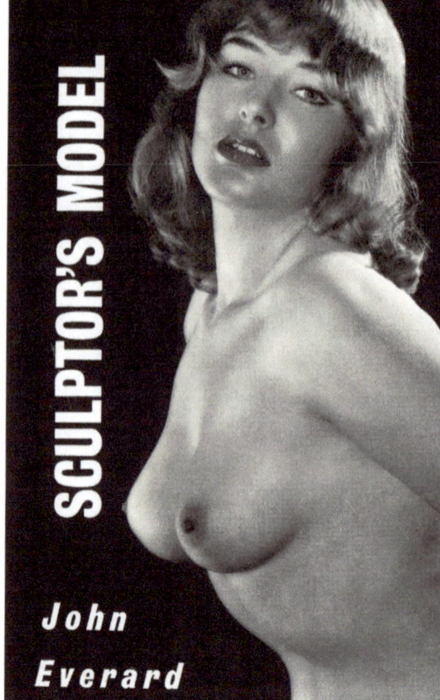

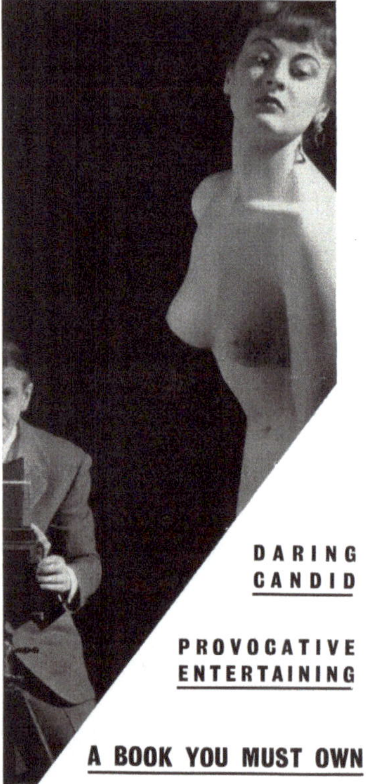

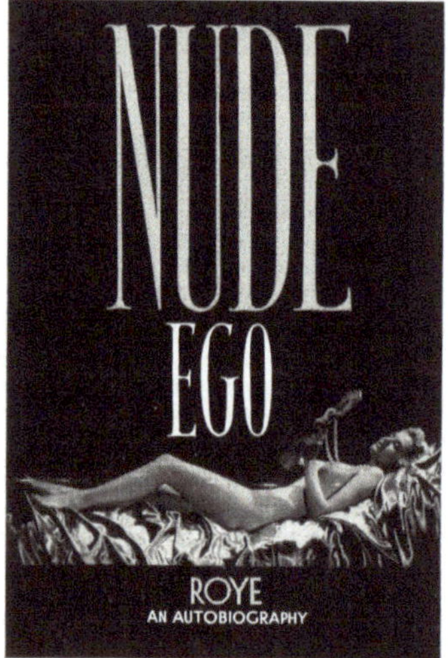

PUBLISHED BY HUTCHINSON

Illustrated jacket, luxuriously bound full-colour frontispiece, 222 pages plus 130 photographs on heavy art paper.

at your Bookseller 25 - or post free from (in Canada and the U.S.A. $4.00).

THE CAMERA STUDIES CLUB
POLPERRO, CORNWALL, ENGLAND.

EVE UNVEILED

48 Beautiful Photographic Studies
by
PHILIP GOTLOP

These forty-eight charming nude studies were all taken out-of-doors in the month of April. They consist of different studies of five girls and each study has been carefully thought out in order to deviate as far as possible from any set posing. Naturists will no doubt appreciate the natural and free atmosphere created. The photography is masterly and from a technical point of view the volume should be of great value to students. The intrinsic charm of these beautiful pictures is enhanced by the natural loveliness of the rural surroundings in which many of them were taken.

Crown 4to.   *5s.*

NUDES

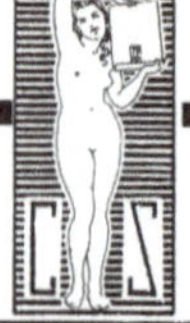

Voted a ' BEST DESIGNED BOOK of 1959 ' by the National Book League.

60 Plates, 11″ × 8½″

OF

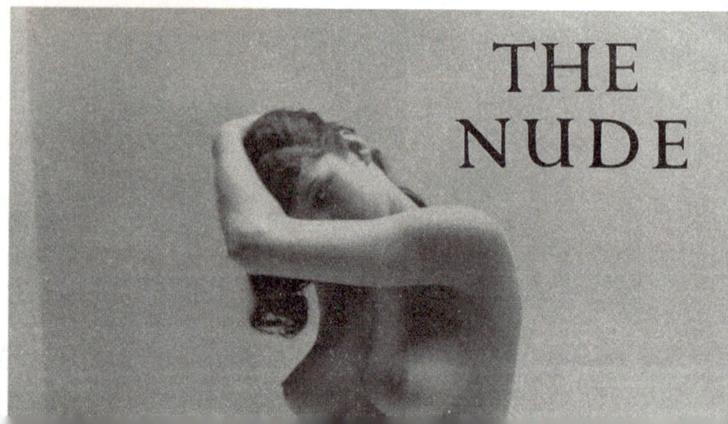

TABLE OF CONTENTS

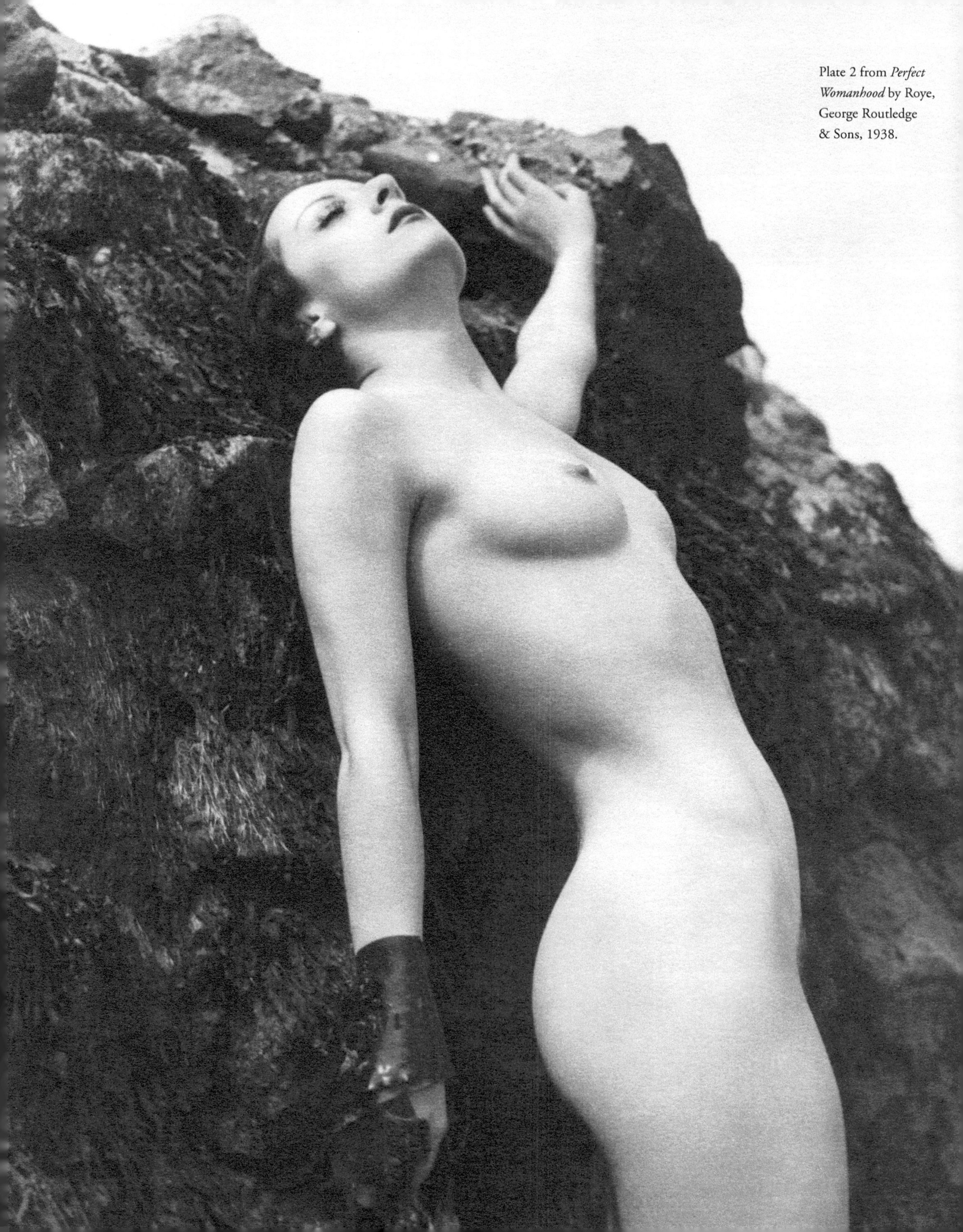

Plate 2 from *Perfect Womanhood* by Roye, George Routledge & Sons, 1938.

Introduction

THE BOOK'S PURPOSE

This book is an annotated bibliography: that is to say, it is a list of books, together with a description of each of them.

Specifically, the bibliography attempts to list all the hardback books which were (a) collections of photographs of the nude and (b) published in England between 1896 and 1960. Such a book cannot claim to be a proper history of photography of the nude – and it is definitely not a collection of actual images.

The starting date for the bibliography, 1896, marks the earliest publication, so far as I can discover, of a book of the kind described. The closing date, 1960, is more arbitrary; but, as will be explained below, the 1960s saw significant changes in attitudes towards nudity and sexuality in general. For these reasons I find it useful to think of the years from the invention of photography until about 1960 as the 'classical' era of nude photography in England.

The overall purpose of this bibliography is to provide information that will be useful to anyone who is interested in photography of the nude. In particular, the book is intended to be of value to collectors, book dealers, librarians and historians. It may also provide some amusing insights into the bizarre pruderies of the English.

The books listed are now becoming both scarce and sought-after. Titles that I bought ten or twenty years ago for £5 or £10 are now being advertised at £80 or £100. The list should, therefore, be of particular value to the collector, who may wish to know as much as possible about a book before parting with a considerable sum of money.

The approach to the subject is scholarly, but the overall tone of the discussion is not, I hope, pompous or unduly serious.

HISTORICAL BACKGROUND

Photography may be said to have been invented in the 1830s, and almost immediately it was used to record images of the naked human body – usually the female body. Some such images were made in France in the 1840s, and the first Englishman known to have tackled the subject was a certain G. Watson, in 1856. Even in 1830 there was, of course, a long and respectable tradition of painting the nude, both male and female; and to some extent the new photographic process could be seen as a continuation of an already well-established practice in European art. However, the use of photography to produce images of the unclothed human body was not universally welcomed. It was inevitable (and, some would argue, natural) that photographic images of the nude should arouse erotic feelings, at last to some degree; but in the mid-nineteenth century, as today, sex and eroticism made some people nervous.

The situation was further omplicated by the rapid development of crude pornography – by which I mean the sale of totally uninhibited pictures of people having sex. Within a very few years of the invention of the new photographic processes, every kind of sexual activity, however sordid, was being depicted. By 1860, art and photography magazines regularly made reference to the 'immoral' photographs which were keeping the law courts busy.

A few years later, in 1874, police raided the London Borough of Pimlico studio of a Mr Henry Hayler and confiscated 130,248 obscene photographs. Mr Hayler evidently used his wife and his two sons as models. Many nineteenth-century Englishmen found that sort of thing distasteful and unacceptable, and they decided, not surprisingly perhaps, that it should be illegal. But that judgement made life difficult for those photographers who were, in their own estimation at least, genuinely trying to produce what they considered to be works of art: beautiful images of beautiful bodies.

In short, the early photographers of the nude were immediately faced with a problem, and it is one which has persisted right up to the present day. The problem is that a sizeable number of people consider that even the most innocuous display of human flesh is disgusting, improper, and should be banned. And this is probably as good a place as any to mention an important consequence of this nineteenth-century prudery. I refer to the conspiracy to eliminate pubic hair. Or more strictly speaking, the determined attempt on the part of the powers that be to pretend that pubic hair did not exist.

THE ANGUISH OVER PUBIC HAIR

It is a curious, and perhaps also a little-known fact, that for the whole of the nineteenth century and until about 1965, the legal authorities in England applied a solitary test to decide whether or not a photograph of a nude woman was obscene. The test was this: is her pubic hair visible? If there was so much as a wisp of the black stuff discernible under a magnifying glass, then the photographer, printer, bookseller, and anyone else whom the police could lay hands on, were all liable to do a stretch in Dartmoor, prison which in the nineteenth century was no fun at all.

I refer to the situation light-heartedly, but in reality it was no joke. The danger of being convicted of publishing obscene material on the strength of this bizarre test was very real.

An article in the *Sunday Times* in 1970 stated that at one time, no fewer than thirty civil servants, with the aid of ten Acts of Parliament, were dedicated to ensuring that pubic hair never appeared in a published photograph. This duty was the responsibility of Customs and Excise Department PT4; PT represents Purchase Tax. As Bill Jay once wrote, 'Why PT4 dealt with such matters is one of our more sinister official secrets.'

Photographers soon developed several solutions to this problem, and these continued to be used until about 1965. One was to ask the model to shave herself. Another was to persuade the model to dye her pubic hair blonde, so that it was less visible when photographed. Finally, in the case of photographs which were printed in magazines and books, it was common for the printer's retouching department to airbrush the hair out of the picture. This latter practice was not only common but crude, and many fine printed images from the years prior to 1965 are marred by an ugly blur across the model's crutch.

Some photographers preferred to take additional precautions. Eva Grant, who was active as a professional photographer in the 1950s, told me that where there was any doubt in her mind, she got her lawyer to vet the print, and to stamp it on the back as conforming with the law. Some took even more extreme precautions. For example, I have in my own collection a print from the 1950s showing the famous model Lorraine Burnett. In it, not only is the lovely Lorraine shaved to within an inch of her life, but the original vendor decided that it was too risky even to show the line between the model's labia. He, or she, took a scalpel, and actually *scraped the surface of the photograph*, if you please, to remove all traces of the fact that this woman possessed any genital organs.

For several decades, the authorities' bizarre attempt to keep pubic hair a secret seems to have caused little comment. It was, after all, a common convention in European painting to cover the genitals with fig leaves, flowing pieces of material, or a chaste hand. Where the female groin was exposed, the convention both in art and sculpture was to portray the area accurately, as far as shape was concerned, but to omit any representation of the short and curly elements, or even the labial divide.

This convention in art may, perhaps, have had something to do with the social mores of classical Greece and Rome. In these ancient civilisations, it was reportedly common for ladies to remove their pubic hair, either by singeing it off with a brand from the fire or by plucking it out with tweezers. Neither method sounds very comfortable; but, let's face it, the ladies have always been willing to suffer to be beautiful.

In any event, whatever the origins of the practice, it is readily observable that, in both paintings and sculpture, the art world has historically avoided realistic depictions of pubic hair; and photography, in the early days, was forcibly prevented from revealing the stuff, whether the photographers and their models wanted to or not.

Attitudes began to change, both in England and elsewhere, in the 1950s. In that decade, there emerged a substantial number of people who thought that this whole approach to pubic hair was ridiculous. Chief among these was the photographer Roye, and I shall give details of how he challenged the authorities when I describe his 1960 publication *Unique Verdict*.

It must also be remembered that in the 1950s there were literally millions of sexually active men who had spent five or six years of their lives fighting Hitler. Such men did not take kindly to being told, by some halfwit in Whitehall, that they couldn't look at a naked woman if they wanted to. As the decade progressed, and as prosperity returned, these men had money in their pockets. By the end of the 1950s, substantial numbers of them were buying unretouched Swedish magazines in Soho, and patronising the strip clubs which came into being at about that time. It gradually became obvious, even to the dimmest prude, that the official line could not be held.

In the early 1960s, the British government (through the Home Office) made it known that bona fide nudist (or naturist) magazines would not be prosecuted if they showed photographs of human beings as nature had created them. In other words, pubic hair – having once been anathema – was now to be permitted.

This change of heart was greeted with relief by fine-art photographers, and for the pornographers, it became a licence to print money. The ruling proved to be the tiny crack in the dam which soon widened to produce an unstoppable flood. Within a few years, every magazine on the newsstand was showing unretouched nudes.

THE CUT-OFF YEAR FOR THIS BIBLIOGRAPHY

As mentioned above, this bibliography ends at the year 1960. There are two principal reasons for that. First, the forces of prudery had by then lost the pubic-hair battle, at least in principle, though the full effects would not be seen for a few years yet. And second, colour printing was becoming much cheaper than it had been in the past.

During the 1960s, photographers, magazine editors, and book publishers, all began to adopt a different approach to photography of the nude. In earlier decades, it had been necessary not only to remove pubic hair from view but also to pose the nude model in a careful, graceful way, so that you could claim to be creating a noble work of art. If you didn't do that, you were likely to end up in prison; and you might end up in trouble even if you did take these precautions.

However, from around 1965 onwards, and certainly by the end of the sixties, all the photographer needed to do was say to the model, 'Drop your knickers, darling, and spread your legs.' And they did so. By the thousand. Photographers and models alike. Furthermore, the new printing technology allowed you to display the hideous results of this practice in full technicolour, complete with blue eye-shadow and pink lipstick. And the law couldn't touch you at all.

In the late 1960s, the products of this changed approach began to be seen in the newsagents' shops. And they can still be seen on the top shelf of W.H. Smith's today: images which are badly posed, badly lit, and badly photographed; they are printed, for the most part, with skin tones of slaughterhouse red.

Thus it was that in 1960, or soon afterwards, what I have referred to as the classical age of English nude photography began to come to an end. We then entered what I think of as the gynaecological era of photography, and gynaecological photography is an art form in which I am not interested. The fine-art style of black and white photography of the nude would continue, of course; but henceforth it was to be a minority interest.

EARLY REACTIONS TO THE PROBLEM OF OBSCENITY

Before I end this introduction, it will be useful if we go back to the first few decades in the lifetime of photography and take note of how the early photographers of the nude dealt with those elements of society which regarded their work as undesirable, at best, or criminal, at worst.

In his 1971 book *Views on Nudes*, Bill Jay makes the point that the early pioneers in this field can be regarded as placing themselves, more or less deliberately, into one of three categories.

First, there were the out-and-out pornographers, such as Mr Hayler, who was mentioned above. The pornographers' interest in the nude was purely commercial. They sought to exploit the shock-horror reaction which was generated by their hardcore pictures; they charged their customers heavily for the privilege, and they tried to evade the law for as long as possible.

Then there was a group of photographers who saw themselves, rightly or wrongly, as being utterly respectable; indeed they regarded themselves as dedicated artists in a high intellectual tradition. We might reasonably call this group the fine-art photographers. Their task, as they saw it, was to create beautiful images which would give harmless pleasure to the viewer. Photographers in this class would have been deeply resentful of anyone who confused them with the pornographers.

Some photographers in this second group achieved full social acceptance. Oscar Gustave Rejlander, a Swede who lived and worked in England, produced a nude composite image called 'The Two Ways of Life', and he even managed to sell a print to Queen Victoria! Indeed, when I visited the Queen's country home, Osborne House, I was astonished by the extent to which Victoria and her husband had filled their rooms with paintings and sculpture of the nude. In Prince Albert's bathroom, for example, the wall immediately above the bath was filled by a picture of a rather luscious young woman, entirely sans covering.

Finally, we can identify a third category among the photographers of the nude in the nineteenth century. The motives of this third group were mainly commercial, I suspect, but they were intellectually a cut above the pornographers, and they recognised that the danger of prosecution was very real.

This group sought to protect themselves by declaring that the images of the nude which they offered for sale were intended entirely for the student of art. Their photographs were – goodness me yes, they definitely were – nothing more or less than anatomical studies for use by the impoverished painter who could not afford to hire a model of his own.

And since, at that time, Art was universally held to be a Good Thing, it followed that no reasonable person could possibly take exception to the provision of practical aids to art students. Could they? True, some of the 'students' who bought these images might not actually be genuine – but that wasn't the photographer's fault, now was it?

It will be useful to bear these three categories in mind as we work through the list of books published between 1896 and 1960. The pornographers, of course, never made it into the respectable world of book publication; and, as we shall see, the practice of labelling collections of nude studies as 'aids for students of art' continued well into the 1950s. But it would be many years before any photographers would dare to suggest that they were providing photographs of beautiful women purely for the pleasure of the viewer.

SOURCES

Much of the research on which this book is based was done some twenty years ago, before the advent of digital databases. I have, however, taken advantage of modern technology to check and add to my information where possible.

The data were initially compiled from standard reference books: the *British National Bibliography; the British Museum Catalogue of Printed Books; British Books in Print; the Cumulative Book Index;* and the *Catalogue of the London Library.* More recently, supplementary information has been obtained from online sources: the British Library Public Catalogue (BLPC); COPAC, which includes the BLPC and for good measure adds the combined catalogues of 24 leading UK universities; OCLC's WorldCat; the Library of Congress database; various books on the history of photography; and booksellers' catalogues, both printed and online. These sources do not often feature in the bibliography, but they are usually abbreviated when they do; a list of abbreviations is provided at the end of this introduction.

DATA PROVIDED

Books are listed by year, beginning in 1896, and alphabetically by author within each year. Each entry gives, as a minimum: the author's surname, followed by the first name; the title of the book; and the publisher. Where I am able to give the size of the book, it is stated in inches, the height being followed by the width. Books are listed at their first publication if possible, though some books reappear in the printed bibliographic sources in later years when they were reissued. The real names of photographers who used pseudonyms are given, where known, at their first appearance. In almost all the books listed, the images were printed as they had originally been photographed, in black and white. The exceptions are noted.

The place of publication, meanwhile, was almost invariably London; again, I have noted any known exceptions. It was, of course, perfectly possible to publish books elsewhere in the United Kingdom, but publishers in other parts of the country rarely traded in nudes. The reason for this was religious sensibilities: during the years covered by this bibliography, Scottish culture was dominated by Presbyterians, whereas the leaders of Welsh society were mostly chapelgoers who closed the pubs on Sundays and didn't allow much fun on any other day of the week either. And in Northern Ireland, books of nude photographs could never be published because that would have been deemed disgusting and immoral.

ISSUES OF CONSISTENCY

The bibliographic sources are sometimes inconsistent in what they include, what they exclude, and what information they provide. I have therefore faced certain problems in deciding what to list here and what to omit.

A hardback book is the embodiment of a photographer's work in a form more permanent than that of a magazine or newspaper; and the principal aim here, as stated above, is to list all hardback books on photography of the nude which were published within the given timeframe. However, the BNB and the BMC both list items which at first appear to be books but which, on examination, prove to be something else.

For instance, the BMC lists *Études Moderne* (sic) by glamour photographer Harrison Marks in just the same way as if it were a hardback publication comparable to his 1956 book *Pamela*. But in fact, the former item is just a 32-page booklet, with a card cover, measuring 7 in by 5 in. For my part, I have omitted all items listed in the sources when I know that they are not, in fact, hardback books.

Another problem arises in relation to books which were originally published in the USA. In the book trade as a whole, it has often been the case that an American book has been formally republished in a British edition by a British firm, even to the extent of redesigning the book and resetting the type.

However, this kind of 'republishing' appears to have happened rarely in relation to the photographic works dealt with here. It seems to have been much more common for a British publisher to have imported a small number (possibly as few as 50) of the American publisher's edition and to have acted as the UK distributor. In some instances this process seems to have been enough to secure a book's listing in the BNB as being 'published' by a UK firm. Where a book appears to have been treated in this way, I have included a note.

WORKS EXCLUDED

Books which deal specifically with nudism (which some enthusiasts prefer to call naturism) are for the most part excluded from this list. However, some such works undoubtedly included photographs by leading photographers of the nude. For example, William Welby's *Naked and Unashamed* (1934) contained studies by Walter Bird and others. Similarly, collections of general photographic work, such as the annual *Photograms of the Year*, often included one or two nudes, but not enough to secure the listing of the book here.

UNRECORDED PUBLICATIONS – A WORD OF WARNING

It might be thought that the hardback books listed here represent the cream of the photographic output of the nude in their era, and that the study of them will provide a true guide as to what was considered the 'best' work during the period in question. But there are dangers in this assumption. It should be noted that many important and successful photographers never had their work published in hardback form. Photographs by Stephen Glass and Eva Grant, for example, never appeared in hardback covers, except in the company of others in the *Photo-art Portfolio of Beauty*. Other distinguished practitioners seem to have confined their work to exhibitions, without trying very hard to achieve publication. One such photographer was Rosalind Maingot, who was a Fellow of the Royal Photographic Society (RPS) and exhibited regularly. I understand that the RPS has 2,000 examples of her work.

Similarly, the student of nude photography should be aware that hardback books were expensive and were beyond the purse of the average man. From about 1935 to 1955, the main market for photographers of the nude, and the main source of such images for consumers, was the monthly nudist/naturist magazine *Health and Efficiency*. The men's magazines *Lilliput* and *Men Only* also carried one or two discreet nude studies in each issue.

This situation began to change in about 1955. In the late 1950s and early 1960s, substantial numbers of pocket-sized publications were issued which were not recorded in the BNB and BMC, or anywhere else. These booklets, which contained photographs of the nude and little else, were often no more than 32 pages in length, plus a card cover; they were sold through newsagents rather than through the book trade.

Although they are often referred to as magazines, and in some cases they appeared in a numbered sequence at monthly intervals, they often lacked a date. The most famous of these publications is perhaps Harrison Marks's *Kamera* series, which ran to at least 86 issues in the late '50s and early '60s.

The total sales of the *Kamera* series alone must number many millions. Thus, the historian should beware of assuming that hardback books, in and of themselves, give an accurate picture of the preferred style and taste of the time. Sometimes, as in the case of Park and Gregory's 1930s works, the books may reasonably be said to be breaking new ground. In other cases, for instance that of Harrison Marks, the photographer's hardback books were simply preserving, in a more permanent form, examples of work which had already proved to be commercially successful.

ABBREVIATIONS

FIRST AND SECOND EDITIONS

The first edition of this book was published in trade paperback form in 2005. It is now out of print, though occasional copies can be found for sale from book dealers.

The second edition incorporated a number of pieces of new information which were provided by readers of the first. The most notable contributor was the model and one-time partner of Harrison Marks, the late Pamela Green. The second edition was respectfully dedicated to her memory [as is the third edition]. I regret now that, in my original text, I referred to her as having 'an almost perfect figure'. The single word 'perfect' will suffice, I think.

THIRD EDITION

This edition of the book is published by Wolfbait Books, with an all-new layout and the addition of images.

BNB = *British National Bibliography*. This was a list of all the books published in the UK in a given year. At one time the information was only available in printed form, with one large volume being issued per year, and although the material was classified according to the Dewey system, it was not always easy to search for books on a given subject. Modern, computer-based sources of information are infinitely more research-friendly.

BLPC = *The British Library Public Catalogue*. An online source: http://blpc.bl.uk. The catalogue seems to contain all the information which was formerly available in the *British Museum Catalogue of Printed Books*, and it should, theoretically, contain details of every book ever published in the UK.

BMC = *British Museum Catalogue of Printed Books*. In the printed version, this used to come in several sections; each section covered a period of some years. Within each section, there were several volumes listing authors alphabetically within the particular period of years. The print was so small that a magnifying glass was needed to read it. The new online version of this British Library catalogue (http://blpc.bl.uk) is, once again, infinitely easier to use.

COPAC = The combined online catalogue of the Consortium of University Research Libraries: the online address is http://www.copac.ac.uk/copac. This database includes the BLPC and more besides.

BIBLIOGRAPHY

1896

✦ A Handbook of Anatomy for Art Students

Thomson, Arthur, Clarendon Press, Size 9" x 6"

This book only just merits inclusion in a bibliography of collections of nude photographs, and it scrapes in for a variety of reasons.

First, this is — so far as I am aware — the earliest book published in England which contains even a few photographs of naked men and women, and it is noteworthy for that reason alone. The halftone process, by which photographs are reproduced in books and magazines, was invented in the 1880s, and only came into general use in newspapers and magazines in the 1890s. So it would have been impossible even to consider printing a book like this much earlier because the technology simply was not available.

There was, of course, another problem, which was that the late Victorian era was profoundly prudish; and so the decision to include photographs of the unclothed human body (in addition to the more chaste line drawings) was a bold one: it could probably only have been made in connection with a book written by the Professor of Human Anatomy in the University of Oxford. And in order to leave the reading public in no doubt whatever about the author's absolute respectability, his title of Professor is printed on the spine of the book as well as on the title page.

Another reason for including the book in this bibliography is that it actually is a genuine book about human anatomy, and it truthfully was intended for use by art students. This makes it almost unique among a host of works making similar but entirely spurious claims. As we shall often see in the pages which follow, the statement that photographs of nudes are being presented 'for use by art students' will often be made over the next 50 or 60 years, but it seldom has any justification: it is usually just an indicator of deep-seated hypocrisy on the part of the author and publisher, coupled with a very natural wish to avoid a prison sentence. This book, however, contains 405 pages of text and goes into enormous scholarly detail on all aspects of human anatomy.

And what of the illustrations? Well, there are 29 pages of plates, interspersed among the text, together with a great number of line drawings. The photographs mostly feature men, with the genital organs painted out, and pictures of women are rare. The majority of photographs are of parts of the body only.

For a collector who is interested in photography of the nude, this is probably not a book which is worth buying. It is, however, a book worth knowing about.

In all, there were five editions of the book, and later editions seem to have included a larger number of plates. Dover published a facsimile of the fifth edition (1929) in the USA in 1964. The book must have sold in substantial numbers because secondhand copies are still easy to come by and at modest prices.

It is worth noting, by the way, that the Germans were not as prudish as the English. In 1900 Dr C.H. Stratz (later, I believe, Professor Stratz) published a book entitled *Die Schönheit des Weiblichen Korpers* – 'The Beauty of the Female Body'. This book, as you might expect from a German author, was a learned and scholarly attempt to analyse and systematise the features and proportions which make a woman beautiful.

Most importantly, from our point of view, Dr Stratz's tome included numerous unretouched photographs of naked women and girls. There were also, of course (since this is a German book we're talking about), plenty of charts and line drawings and graphs, because the Germans are nothing if not thorough.

Dr Stratz's work seems to have found a wide audience – the Germans being well known for their philosophical turn of mind. The book was reissued in a new edition from time to time, the last occasion reportedly being in 1941. English readers would have to wait another 60 years or so before being allowed to see female pubic hair in book form.

1916

✦ Hieroglyphic, or the Greek Method of Life Drawing

Braun, Adolphe Armand, Drawing Ltd

Not seen, but said to be 12" x 9". Card covers and 186 pages. This appears not to be a hardback book, and therefore, according to our somewhat arbitrary rules, should be excluded; but I have left it in as it is such an early example of the nude in printed form.

A bookseller's description says that there are hundreds of drawings and 64 plates featuring a Miss Dorothy Lees as the model. She is mostly nude, though occasionally clothed: as Britannia she wears a helmet and carries both sword and shield. The photographer was E.D. Cooke.

The book seems to have been published by the London School of Drawing, which offered correspondence courses and issued a magazine; it may have been distributed by, or co-published with, Batsford. Later editions (of which there were many) are usually described as being published by the Postal University. The book offers instructions on how to draw the human body, but it seems likely that it was bought more for its illustrations than for its advice.

✦ Studies of the Human Figure, with Some Notes on Drawing and Anatomy

Ellwood, G.M. and Yerbury, F.R., Batsford

This book was not see at the time of preparing this bibliography, but its size is reported as 9" x 7", and it apparently has 28 pages of text, 14 pages of drawings, and either 64 or 80 pages of photographs, depending on which description you believe. One bookseller says that the models are shown 'in a variety of tasteful but strange poses'. The price was 16 shillings; even in the late 1950s, you could buy a 32-page booklet of nudes for two shillings and sixpence, i.e. less than one-sixth of the price of this one.

This is another book for 'the use of Students and Artists', at least according to the publisher's advertisement for it. The book is claimed to consist of 'A series of large-scale Reproductions of 80 Artistic Photographic Studies from Male, Female and Child models.' (The capital letters are in the original title) F.R. Yerbury was chiefly an architectural photographer, and he is identified as Secretary of the Architectural Association; this post is not obviously relevant to the book, but it serves to indicate how desperate the publisher was to establish the respectability of the authors.

Writing in the *Manchester Weekly Times*, Mr Garnett, Head Art Master at the Manchester Grammar School, described the book as 'an almost sumptuous publication... unique in conception and treatment'. This may have been true by the standards of the time. However, I once saw a copy in a secondhand bookshop, and, unless my memory is defective, the images were small, badly printed by modern standards, and not remarkable except that they were among the earliest pictures of naked men and women to appear between hard covers in the United Kingdom.

Later editions appeared in 1921 and 1924. In 1927, incidentally, Mr Yerbury was the co-author, with a Mr Cornford, of a book entitled *Roedean School*! Now there's a happy thought. But it was, I imagine, a study of the school's architecture.

✦ The Garden of Adonis

Hill, Oliver, Philip Allan

Not seen, but said to be about 12" x 9¾". In the past I have occasionally seen this book advertised, but I have never been tempted to buy it. Why? Because it features photographs of nude children.

There are 48 plates in all, and according to one bookseller they show 'idyllic images of nude young children playing in outdoor settings, mostly on the banks of a river'. The photographs are said to illustrate fragments of poems. 'An amazing book,' says another bookseller, 'naive in its conception, but splendidly produced!'

I take leave to doubt whether it was naive in its conception. I have a suspicion that the author knew exactly what he was about, as, I suspect, do modern sellers and buyers of this material. On the day that I'm writing this, five copies are offered for sale on the internet, at prices ranging from £86 to £420.

Should you wish to know more about the author and his book, I gather that *Love in Earnest* by Timothy d'Arch Smith (Routledge, 1970) provides further explication.

It is difficult to make a final judgement about a book without seeing it, but this one seems to be, at best, in rather poor taste; at worst, it may be thoroughly unpleasant.

✦ The Human Form and its Use in Art

Yerbury, F.R. and Crossley, F.H., Batsford

Not seen. 'Prepared for Designers, Students, and Artists', says the publisher's blurb. 'A Series of 118 Photographic Studies on 73 Plates from specially selected Female and Child models, including a special Series of Male Studies by F.H. Crossley, F.S.A. With an Introduction on the Application of the Figure in Decorative Art by G. Montague Ellwood.' The price was 18 shillings, which again was a lot of money in those days.

The BLPC says there are 60 plates and some 47 pages of text. 'Of the plates themselves, one cannot speak too highly,' said the *Journal of Decorative Arts and British Decorator*.

✦ Nature and Culture

Landow, Peter, Chapman and Hall

Not seen, but said to be 12" x 9½". The subtitle is 'Photographs of various nationalities'. A bookseller's catalogue reports that the book contains 120 sepia-toned photographs, each plate featuring a single image, and all of them female nudes; it therefore seems to be a comparative study of various racial and cultural types. The photographs are by a number of different hands.

For several years we have had 'studies for art students', but now we have a new dodge: this time the images of naked ladies are justified anthropologically; the author has a PhD, just to reassure us that all is well.

In view of the analytical character of the work, it is perhaps not surprising to find that it was originally published in Berlin (1925); a French edition also exists. According to the BLPC, the English edition was printed in Germany.

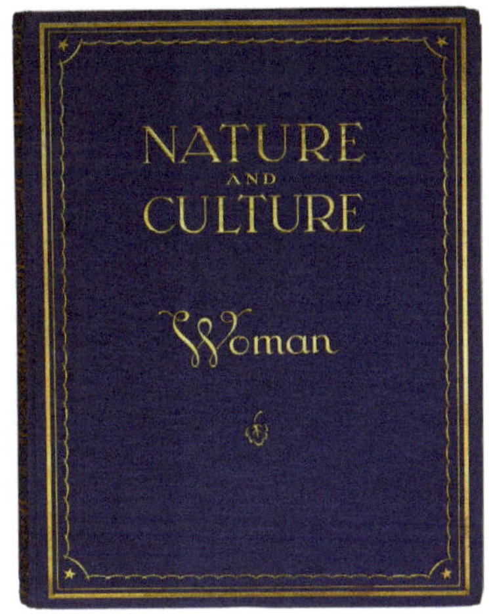

✦ Living Sculpture

Park, Bertram, Gregory, Yvonne, and Ellwood G.M., Batsford, Size 11½" x 9"

Some 32 pages of text and about 60 plates all told, the main section of plates being printed on glossy paper, one side only. Each image has a title, such as 'Penance' and 'Vibrating Light'. The original price is unknown, but it would certainly have been high.

The first thing to be said about this book is that it was a courageous venture. It comes close to being one which presents nudes (nearly all female) for their own sake. But, as would commonly be the case for some decades yet, the publishers still felt it necessary to describe the work as something else: in this case, 'A record of expression in the human figure'. An earnest and superficially learned introduction by G. Montague Ellwood was also added, presumably to give an aura of respectability which might otherwise be lacking.

Ellwood, of course, had been involved in two earlier Batsford books (see above); apart from that, his sole qualification for pontification on the nude seems to have been that he was joint editor of the journal *Drawing*. His introduction to this work covers everything from the Piltdown Man to Russell Flint.

Bertram Park and Yvonne Gregory were a husband and wife team, both of them being photographers, but no indication is given as to who took which shot. The photographs are arranged in groups featuring particular postures, such as Standing, Kneeling, etc, and six discreet male nudes are provided at the end.

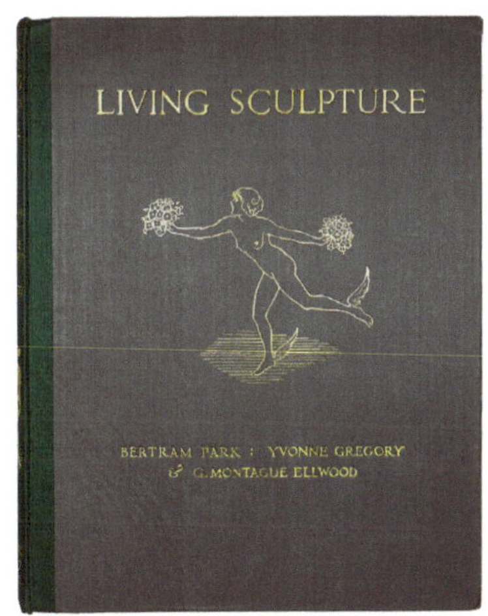

After the introduction there is a section headed 'Notes on the Illustrations'. The note on 'Vanity' says that it is 'a curious pose of stepped angles'. In fact, it is simply a picture of a nude girl sitting on an antique table with one hand over her head.

The models are for the most part attractive and well posed – most of the shots were taken in the studio, but there is a sprinkling of outdoor studies. The printing is also first class by the standards of the day. All in all, a groundbreaking effort and one which, with the benefit of hindsight, deserves high praise.

1928

✦ Pan's Garden

Hill, Oliver, Philip Allan

Not seen, but reported to be 11½" x 9". This is very similar in content to the same author's 1923 book *The Garden of Adonis*. In other words, we have 48 allegedly tasteful photographs of nude children. Each photograph is said to 'illustrate' a passage from Shakespeare or some other poet.

'Considered a classic in its genre,' says one bookseller. No doubt, but it does not appeal to me. Prices on the secondhand market vary from £110 to £345.

1931

✦ The Art of the Body

Agneil, Marguerite, Batsford

Not seen, but said to be 9" x 6". Essentially, this book is about physical fitness, and it provides the reader with a series of exercises incorporating dance, 'Oriental postures' and other fanciful ideas. Various booksellers and databases reveal that there are 114 pages plus 62 plates. The images sometimes show Miss Agneil nude, and sometimes lightly clad.

In 1933 Miss Agneil produced another book, *Body Sculpture*, which was published by E.H. & A.C. Friedrichs of New York. In that book there are 30 pages of Miss Agneil nude. To my eye she is an elegant enough lady, evidently well trained in dance, but in about half of the images she is coated in some kind of bronze body makeup, and heavily oiled besides; this is not an attractive combination.

✦ The Male Body

Unattributed, Routledge, Size 7½" x 5"

A very early, and rare, example of the male nude. The author/photographer, or editor, chose to remain anonymous. This is a small, thin, flimsy little book, possibly designed to be slid into the pocket of a gentleman's jacket without causing him embarrassment. It was originally priced at 2s. 6d. and was part of the 'Seen by the Camera' series, which included such titles as *Negro Types* and *Hollywood As It Really Is*.

The Male Body contains 58 pictures. Many, possibly all, are of the same man, though since some shots feature parts of the body, rather than the whole thing, it is hard to say. All the shots were presumably taken by a single (unnamed) photographer in his studio. The model is usually more or less naked, though there is no hint of a penis anywhere; even the occasional thong or jockstrap is not very well filled.

There is, inevitably, an introduction, which is again unattributed. This one begins with a quotation from Heine and considers the theme 'What has man's body meant for him at various times? Salvation or damnation, a gift from God or a temptation of the Devil?' In six pages the anonymous author moves from 510 BC to the present day, with a mention of the Prussian interest in gymnastics. He argues the case that nudity is all right really, despite what the Christian church says, because the Greeks went in for it and the Greeks were pretty good chaps on the whole.

The introduction is followed by notes on the illustrations by Professor E. Matthias. 'The modelling of the back is beautiful,' says the Prof. of picture 6 (which offers us a rear view of a man shadowboxing), 'and the play of the body with its own shadows is charming.' Hmm... Still, one must not be too cynical or critical, because these early pioneers were undoubtedly putting themselves at risk by becoming associated with a publication of this kind. The book cannot have sold very well, for no one bothered to copy it for many years to come.

◆ The Body Beautiful – Physical Culture for Women

Bloch, Alice, John Lane, Size 10" x 7½"

This book was first published in Germany in 1926, as *Harmonische Schulung des Frauenkörpers* (literally 'the harmonious schooling of women's bodies'). The English version was translated from the sixth German edition by Mathias H. Machery.

The size is half an inch wider than the original German edition. Most of the photographs are common to both editions, but there are a few variations.

In her preface to the sixth edition, Alice Bloch refers to the 'very large public demand for my book'. She tells us that the first edition was well received by the critics and that only a small minority of readers objected to the use of the 'undraped form' in the illustrations.

The general rule is that books on physical culture and nudism are excluded from the present bibliography; however, this one is worth listing for a number of reasons.

First, it is a salutary reminder that the nudist and 'health' movement was becoming surprisingly popular in the 1930s, and the interest in outdoor activities had a distinct bearing on the public's willingness to tolerate printed images of the female nude.

The rise of the philosophy that nude sunbathing and exercise were good for both the body and the soul has been admirably chronicled by Adam Clapham and Robin Constable in *As Nature Intended* (Heinemann/Quixote, 1982). The movement began in Germany, where Heinrich Pudor's book *The Cult of the Nude* was published in the last decade of the nineteenth century. Alice Bloch was a German lady who belonged firmly in this tradition. She wrote a number of books, of which this is the most famous.

The chief characteristic of *The Body Beautiful* is that it contains over a hundred photographs of attractive young ladies undertaking gymnastic exercises in the nude, both indoors and outdoors. To the average Englishman, these photographs must have been – quite literally – an eye-opener. Nothing like them had ever been seen before. The sight of attractive young women, quite naked, bending and stretching themselves into all kinds of interesting positions, is the stuff that dreams are made of. Yet here we have it, in real life. And sometimes there are as many as six girls in the same picture! If this was not one of John Lane's all-time bestsellers then all one can say is that here was a missed opportunity.

Judging by the evidence contained in this book, Alice Bloch must have been a major influence on Mary Bagot Stack, the founder of the British physical-culture organisation that in the 1930s was known as the Women's League of Health and Beauty; its present name is the Fitness League. In 1931 Bagot Stack wrote a book called *Building the Body Beautiful* (Chapman and Hall); the title is remarkably similar to that of the Bloch book and can scarcely be a coincidence. That book was also illustrated with photographs, but regrettably, the models were not naked.

Present-day members of the Fitness League tell me that the illustrations in the Bloch book show a number of exercises which are still taught by the Fitness League today. Indeed one of them, labelled 'Weitsprung', shows a young woman performing a graceful leap into the air with a body posture which in due course became adopted as the League's logo. The League's leap was performed, however, by Peggy St Lo. All of that having been said, I have to report that the history page on the Fitness League's current website makes no mention whatever of any German influence on their revered founder. So either the impact of German methods was indirect, or else it just became too embarrassing to be mentioned after the outbreak of World War II in 1939.

Another reason for including this book in the bibliography is my suspicion that it demonstrated to publishers (a) that there were profits to be made from this kind of image, and (b) that, with care, publication of nude photographs need not necessarily be followed by a period of incarceration at His Majesty's Pleasure. There was an American edition, published in 1932, entitled *Harmonious Development of Women's Bodies*. Same translator.

All in all, this is a most interesting book and a quite remarkable publication for its time.

✦ Sunlight and Studio

Sunlight, Liverpool: Dane and Co.

Not seen. I have been unable to discover anything about this book; however, it is listed in COPAC as containing 'photographs from the nude'. One thing I have been able to discover, though, and which may be relevant, is that, in the 1880s, William Lever invented Sunlight Soap, which was much advertised from that time onwards. Part of the advertisement process included the publication of books, such as the *Sunlight Almanac* of 1896 ('a home treasury of information for the use of all members of a household').

Is it possible that the makers of Sunlight could have produced a book advocating not only the benefits of soap and water, but also the value of fresh air and nude sunbathing? Well, the makers of Sunlight were based in the Liverpool area, where this book was published. And we are in 1933, after all: the passion for fresh air and exercise was at something of a peak, as the previous entry for the Alice Bloch book shows.

✦ The Beauty of the Female Form.

Park, Bertram, and Gregory, Yvonne, Routledge, Size 9¾" x 7½"

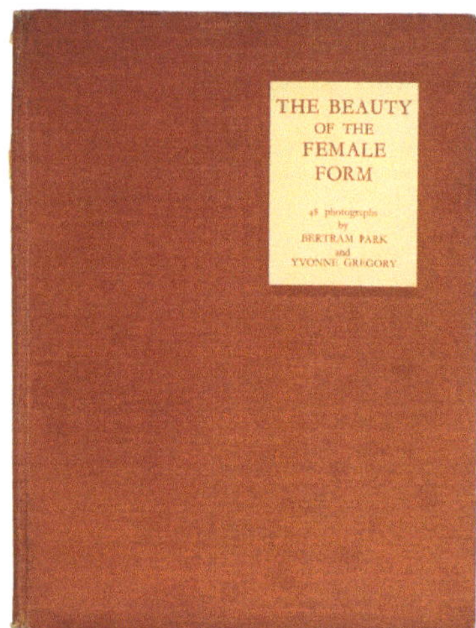

This book was part of Routledge's 'Seen by the Camera' series, which was to prove very popular, as we shall see when we come to consider the work of Roye. The series also included *Horses and Ponies* and *Big Cats and Little Cats*. Much as I love little furry creatures (I will avoid dubious references to pussies), I doubt whether the animal volumes sold as well as the nudes.

Typically, the books in the 'Seen by the Camera' series included 48 pages of plates. This was because photographs needed to be printed on a special glossy paper, and 48 pages was an economical number for a printer to bind in.

In a brief foreword, the husband and wife photographers make the usual attempt to protect themselves from criticism by asserting that these studies will be 'of the greatest use' to the student and artist 'in the composition of their designs'. Yes indeed. They go on to emphasise, lest anyone should suspect that they had taken these pictures just for fun, that the images are 'serious studies' which endeavour to represent 'the gradation of light and shade on the line and mass of the female form in balanced composition'.

There follow seven pages of 'critical annotations', by an unnamed hand, on the 48 pages of plates. Here is an example: 'no artist could miss the aesthetic charm of the exquisite lighting effect of this study.' The plate in question is a fairly standard studio shot of a pleasant enough model.

I am inclined to doubt that Park and Gregory were sufficiently pompous to write this sort of guff themselves, even tongue in cheek, and I suspect that 'an authority' was drafted in by the publisher. He, or she, seems to have demanded anonymity as well as a fee.

The 48 plates are unusually pleasing; some of the images were later reprinted many times in magazines. The early pages are outdoor shots, with the later ones having been taken in the studio. In the good old nineteenth-century tradition, each image has a title, such as 'Despair' or 'Contemplation'. All in all, however, these photographs strike me as an advance on what had appeared earlier. Some of the poses are quite daring, for the period, and some of the models are extremely graceful: one suspects training in dance.

✦ The Body Beautiful

Campbell, Heyworth, ed., British Periodicals Ltd

Not seen, but said to be 11¼" x 8¾" or a bit bigger. This is a slightly mysterious publication which shares the same title as the Alice Bloch book of 1933. Some US references suggest a series of five volumes featuring American photographers, published in 1938 and 1939. Some UK references suggest three or four volumes. I have no evidence that these multiple volumes ever really existed, though a series may well have been planned.

British Periodicals Ltd (listed as publisher) is a name which will crop up again in this bibliography. The company was apparently a subsidiary of the Fountain Press, and, despite the word 'periodicals', seems to have either published or distributed books. Their name is most often found in relation to books on photography.

In any event, the Library of Congress tells us (as do many US booksellers) that there was a US publication with this author and title issued by the Dodge Publishing Company of New York in c.1935. It had an introduction by Dorothy Cocks (and no, I did not make that up). I am fairly confident that the United Kingdom 'edition', allegedly published by British Periodicals, was simply imported from the USA with, perhaps, the name of the 'UK publisher' pasted onto the title page.

The Dodge edition was spiral bound and contained 70 to 90 plates (depending on which description you believe) of female nudes. Campbell seems to have been the editor, rather than the sole photographer, because the book is said to include work by Greeven, Peel, Thayer, Lee, and others.

Heyworth Campbell is known to the BLPC only as the compiler and editor of *Camera Around the World* (Chapman and Hall, 1937).

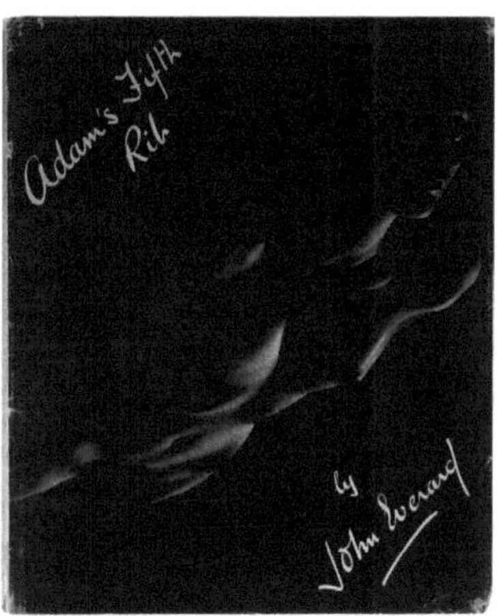

✦ Adam's Fifth Rib

Everard, John (pseudonym for Edward Ralph Forward),
Chapman and Hall, Size 12½" x 10¼"

This is the first of a series of books by John Everard, as he was known professionally. This one, like most of his books, was a handsome production, bound in pale cream linen. The subtitle of this first effort is 'A collection of photographic studies of the nude', which was bold for its time; there is no mention here, you will notice, of 'studies for art students', though John Everard did plenty of that sort of thing later, as we shall see.

The dust jacket of my copy shows a discreet nude, heavily shrouded in shadow. The inside flap tells us that Mr Everard's work will be familiar to readers of *The Bystander*, and that it 'stands apart from his contemporaries for its undeniable originality of treatment' – which is an interesting insight into how it was viewed in its time. The dust jacket also tells us that the images are reproduced in photogravure, which is 'as near as possible the equal of an original print'. In short, no expense was spared in producing this book, and it was doubtless highly priced.

The editor of *The Bystander*, one R.S. Hooper, provides a one-page foreword which is not particularly informative. It tells us, however, that John Everard has a studio in Orange Street, and that he is self-taught. Mr Hooper admits that he himself is wholly ignorant of the mechanics of photography and that he must 'let Mr Everard's enchanting pictures speak for themselves'.

There is no other text, apart from a list of plates giving the title of each study. We then have 48 pages of nudes, one shot to a page, printed on one side of the paper only. Most are of single models, taken in the studio, though a few are outdoors. The models are for the most part young and graceful. Perhaps it goes without saying that they were photographed with skill and care: the publisher would hardly have gone to such trouble otherwise.

All in all, this is an outstanding early example of the classical English style in nude photography. Not so long ago, I read a learned article by a US academic (female at that) which stated that Edward Weston slept with virtually all his models, while Irving Penn kept the subjects of his work 'at a monkish distance'. The difference, the academic lady argued, was apparent in their pictures. For what it is worth, I detect no sign in John Everard's work that he was on intimate physical terms with any of his models. The pictures are far from sexless, but they are chaste, polite, and reserved.

◆ Sun Bathers

Park, Bertram, and Gregory, Yvonne,
Routledge, Size 9¾" x 7½"

Another volume in Routledge's 'Seen by the Camera' series, by the prolific husband and wife team. It is described on the title page as 'A companion volume to *The Beauty of the Female Form*.' The dust jacket features two naked young women beside a swimming pool. This is appropriate, given the title, but it must have been a bold move for its time.

The book has an introduction by one Alan Warwick, who also has some bold things to say. He declares that he speaks 'with some knowledge of the nudist movement' and that 'the beautiful photographs displayed here are... honest windows looking onto the new movement born of an unstable world'. Which was plain speaking indeed, for 1935. The book might be called, he suggests, 'True Freedom'. Every page, he avers, 'speaks in pictures of a freedom that not many dare to possess'.

This introduction marks a distinct change from what has gone before. True, we have had books on the harmonious development of women's bodies and so forth. But this is the first book of photographs to be linked directly to nudism, and the first to make no bones about the fact that being naked can be pleasurable. Some of the models are actually smiling at the camera! My goodness. What is more, the book definitely implies, even if it does not overtly state, that looking at photographs of naked women can be a pleasurable experience too.

Not surprisingly, given the book's title, the 48 plates are all outdoor shots of female nudes, often with more than one model, and sometimes as many as four. The locations vary from open countryside (or a very large garden) to swimming pool and seashore.

As with the previous Park and Gregory book, many of these images would later be reprinted in magazines, notably the nudist journal *Health and Efficiency*. Incidentally, despite that magazine's oft-repeated statement that it was founded in 1900, it did not become associated with nudism, or start to publish nude photographs, until the mid-1930s.

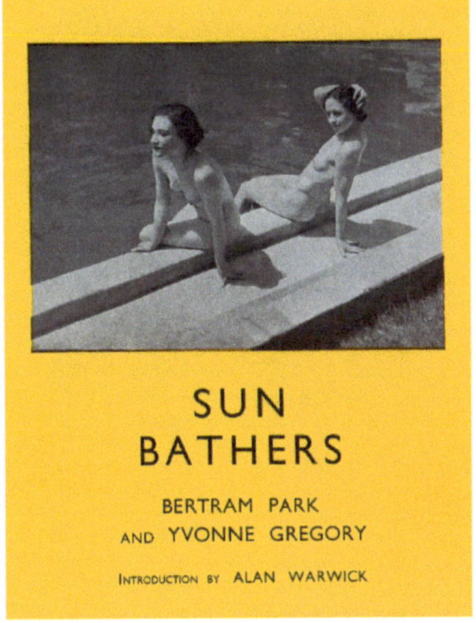

◆ Female Form

Pinchot, Ben,
John Lane

Not seen, but reported to be 10" x 7". Yet another book dedicated to 'the student who must learn to work from a living model, yet cannot afford the mounting expense of retaining one for daily use'. Was this written tongue in cheek, one wonders?

There are 60 pages, and 32 nude photographs, not all of which feature female models (despite the title). There was an American edition published by Bridgeman in the same year, so the book may, in fact, be American in origin.

1936

◆ Life Lines

Everard, John,
Chapman and Hall, Size 12" x 10"

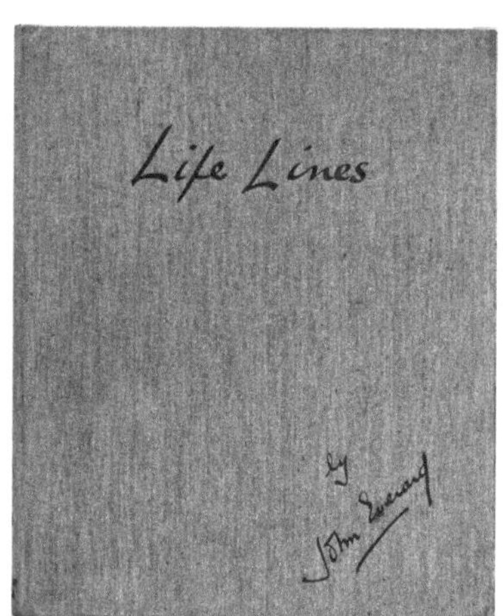

Bound in a kind of coarse linen, possibly cream in colour originally. An impressive-looking book which must have been expensive to print and hence to buy.

In a four-line foreword, John Everard dedicates the book to 'those whose natural grace of mind and body has made it possible.'

There are 48 plates, each printed on one side only of the heavy paper; they mostly fill the page. The majority are studio shots, and of them the majority are low key and employ a soft-focus effect. A number of outdoor studies are included, and they tend to emulate the studio shots in lighting and tone.

I appreciate that the above description does not make the book sound very enticing, but the overall effect of the 48 plates is, oddly enough, rather powerful. This must have been a significant book in its day, and no doubt did much to enhance John Everard's reputation.

✦ Curves and Contrasts of the Human Figure.

Park, Bertram, and Gregory, Yvonne,
John Lane, Size 11" x 8"

This book was also bound in a kind of coarse linen, which makes it similar in appearance to John Everard's volume of the previous year.

Curves and Constrasts comes with an introduction by Professor Bernard Adams, of the Heatherley School of Art, assuring us, as usual, that this collection will 'be of great service to those artists and illustrators who... will want to get below the surface and construct their figures with a knowledge of the forms which actually influence the outer aspect'. Quite. Naturally, no one other than an artist or illustrator would want to look at a book like this.

One could quote other silly statements from the introduction, but it would be wearisome. Suffice it to say that these publishers were not as bold as Chapman and Hall (Everard's publisher in 1935), and considered it necessary to include this kind of tosh in order to protect themselves from criticism.

There are some 80 pages of photographs, reproduced by photogravure, but this time printed on both sides of the paper. The husband and wife team seem to have favoured rather heavier women than John Everard, and the images, therefore, have a more voluptuous air. Indeed some of them might almost be called abandoned. Dear me, the world was going to hell in a handcart. But then it was the 1930s, after all.

✦ Shadowless Figure Portraiture

Peel, Fred P.,
British Periodicals

Not seen, but reported to be about 12" x 9¼". COPAC has no record of this book or the author. Mr Fred Peel certainly had a book of this title published in New York (Galleon Press, c.1936), and so the probability (as with the Heyworth Campbell book of 1935), is that British Periodicals simply imported a few copies. The US edition was spiral bound, with 61 plates of nudes and various chapters on technique

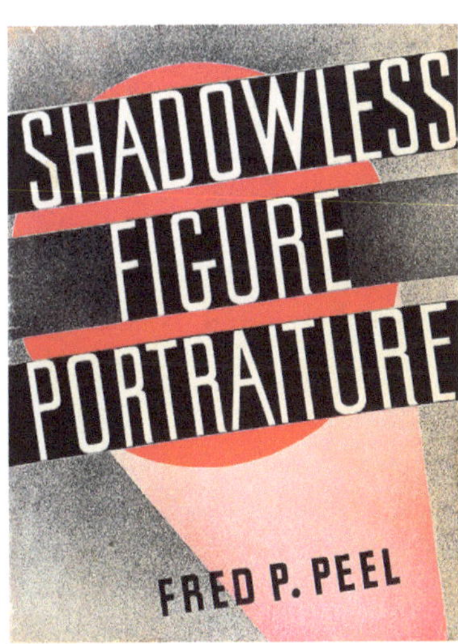

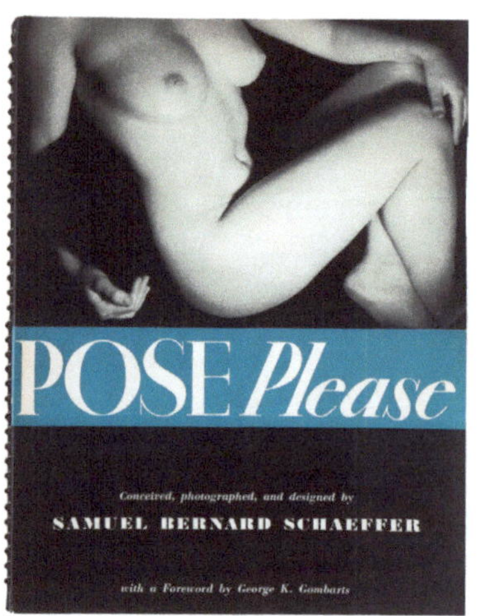

✦ Pose Please

Schaeffer, Samuel Bernard,
British Periodicals

Not seen but reportedly 12" x 9¾". One bookseller says the size is 15" x 12", but he may not have been sober.

The Library of Congress catalogue tells us that *Pose Please* was published by Knopf in New York and London. So what British Periodicals have to do with it I don't quite know; as with the Peel book, above, they were probably importers and distributors. (See the same photographer's *Morning, Noon, Night*, of 1937.)

The book contains more than 100 photographs; many are nudes, but there are also sections on various subjects from infants to hands and feet. The book is clearly intended to be 'an aid to artists'.

✦ Nudes of all Nations

Unattributed,
Routledge,
Size 11" x 7¼"

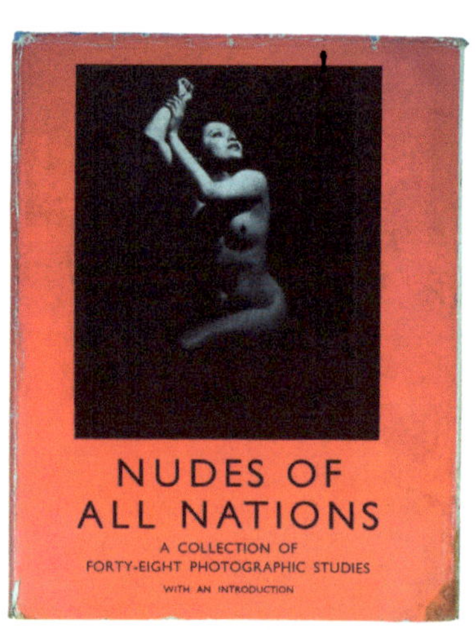

Part of the 'Seen by the Camera' series. The foreword, unsigned, tells us that the purpose of the collection is 'to provide as wide as possible a variety of national types of female beauty', and it adds that more than half of the images are of women from Africa, Asia, the Far East, and the Pacific Islands. A contents list at the front identifies the models by nationality, and the name of the photographer is shown under each picture.

Some familiar names appear among the photographers: Walter Bird, Perkhammer, John Everard, Hoppé, and Manassé are there several times. Though I doubt whether the High Commissioner for New Zealand really took the photograph of the two nude Maori girls.

This seems to have been a popular book: it was reprinted in 1937, 1939, and 1940.

✦ Living Colour

Everard, John,

Routledge, but see below, Size 11½" by 8½"

Examples of nudes reproduced in colour are rare in this list; this is the earliest. In my copy, the title page identifies the publisher as the Dodge Publishing Company of New York. The name and address of Routledge is printed on a slip of paper which has been pasted in, leaving the name of Dodge visible underneath. This might indicate that the book was imported, but on the other hand the copyright page states that the book was printed in Great Britain.

John Everard writes his own introduction. He deals mainly with the technical aspects of working in colour, and explains that he used Dufaycolor films. He then goes on to discuss some of the problems of composition. There follow 24 colour plates, each on the right-hand page, with the reverse left blank. On the left-hand page, opposite each image, is a diagram representing the overall shape of the composition. Underneath each diagram is some information about the lens used, the aperture, and the length of exposure. This arrangement of technical data and image means that between each set of printed pages there are two blank pages.

Perhaps the most surprising aspect of this book is not the colour but the fact that Everard sometimes uses two, three, or four models in the same shot. For its time, the quality of the printing is excellent.

✦ Beauty in the Human Form

Gaston and Andrée,

Gaston and Andrée, Size 10½" x 8½"

The book has a spiral wire binding, which should, theoretically, allow the pages to lie flat, but on my copy the binding is rather tight and a little rusty.

Gaston and Andrée were a famous pair of cabaret dancers, much noted for their daring act which, if the pictures are anything to go by, involved complete or near nudity. They published this book themselves, the illustrations being taken by Walter Bird and a couple of others.

There is a list of plates, 32 in number, and a two-page introduction, unsigned. It tells us that Rosemary Andrée was almost as famous for winning the title of 'Britain's Venus' as for her dancing. The images are all printed on the right-hand page, with a title and a few words of explanation on the left. Physically, Rosemary Andrée was petite, and Monsieur Gaston (as he was known) was no giant either, but both were, of course, superb specimens. There are some shots of each dancer solo, and some of them together.

Gaston's career as a dancer came to a premature end when he fell off the front of a stage, into the orchestra pit. I am told by a performer friend that this is all too easy to do, because when on stage you are often blinded by the lights from on high. After his fall Gaston aged rapidly. His partner went on to have a successful career as a performer's agent, specialising in strippers. In the 1960s she represented many of the girls who worked at the Raymond Revuebar in London's Soho and the Casino de Paris.

✦ Highlights and Shadows

Genthe, Arnold (editor),

Thorsons, Size 11¾" x 9"

This book was American in origin, and was published by Greenberg in New York. The book is not listed in the BLPC or COPAC, so it seems likely that Thorsons simply imported and distributed a few copies.

Highlights and Shadows is yet another example of spiral binding, with a black plastic binder rather than wire. The pages are unnumbered, but there are some 90 to 100 'artistic photographs' of nudes, with technical data. A large number of different photographers and styles are represented, and the print quality of the images is good.

Most of the photographers appear to be American; there are one or two shots of male models; and the editor himself provides a few images. Fascinatingly, there is also one shot by Thomas H. Uzzell, who was chiefly famous as the author of some excellent books on the technique of writing fiction.

All in all, a pretty good collection for its time, though it is obviously of more interest to collectors of American work rather than English.

✦ My Best Nude Study

Jay, Francis, ed.,
Routledge, Size 9¾" x 7½"

A collection of the 'best' work of 48 different photographers. Francis Jay is not, strictly speaking, the author of this book, or even the editor; he is the author of the foreword only. My copy is dated 1941, without any hint that the book had been published earlier, and there was evidently a 1939 edition too.

The foreword tells us that 'the finest examples of the rendering of the nude were made in the best period of ancient Greek art', and goes on to discuss the work of most, if not all, of the 48 photographers involved. The list includes many representatives from the UK, but also several from continental countries, such as Hungary and France.

The pictures are printed on both sides of the paper and are tolerably well reproduced. All but a dozen are studio shots. One shot is by Joan Craven, who was an excellent but rarely published English photographer.

✦ The Model

Mortensen, William,
San Francisco: Camera Craft Publishing Company, Size 9¾" x 6¾"

Strictly speaking, this book does not belong in the bibliography, since it was published in the USA. There is, however, a copy in the British Library, and it is possible that some copies were imported by Fountain. A second edition was published in the USA in 1948. Mortensen was a painstaking practitioner and theorist, and his books are known to have influenced English photographers; *The Model* is listed here for that reason.

The book (262 pages) consists mostly of text, and not all the illustrations are of nudes, by any means. Enormous emphasis is placed on posing the model gracefully.

I gather, from various references in newsgroups etc, that Mr Mortensen is no longer universally admired. However, he was certainly a classy photographer of nudes, and managed to persuade or instruct his models to adopt remarkably graceful poses. Vintage prints of his nudes sell for high prices: the last one I enquired about was available for $2,500.

✦ Photography of the Nude

Natkin, M.,
Fountain, Size 10¾" x 7¼"

Natkin, first name Marcel, was presumably French. There was a French edition, published by Éditions Mana, in Paris, in 1937, and, as detailed below, the contributors seem to have been mostly French.

This book, which runs to 38 pages of text and 32 plates, is not so much a collection of nudes as a collection of short essays on various aspects of nude photography and the work of specific photographers.

The first chapter deals with the nude in painting and sculpture and provides a very rapid survey of art from antiquity to the author's own day. Natkin then gives us brief introductions to the work of four photographers: Laure Albin Guillot, Pierre Boucher, Man Ray, and Roger Schall. For the most part these are avant-garde workers, Man Ray of course being associated with the Surrealist movement. At the end there is a technical section, giving details of lighting, soft-focus techniques, and so on.

✦ Eve in the Sunlight

Park, Bertram, Gregory, Yvonne,
Hutchinson, Size 11" x 8"

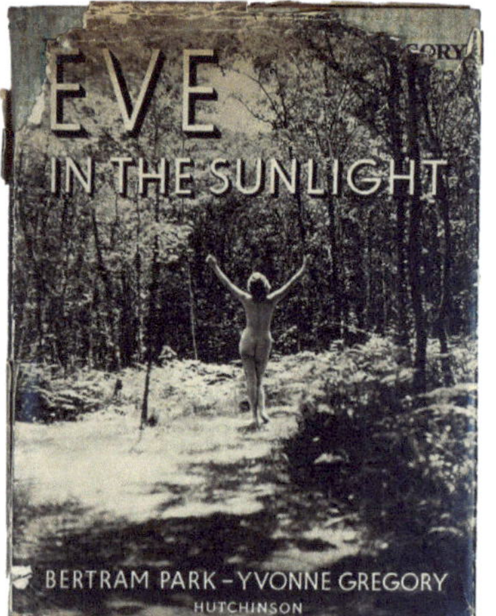

With an introduction by Alan Warwick, who rambles a good deal, but does make a couple of interesting points. The first is that this present set of pictures by Park and Gregory marks a departure from the practice of giving images solemn titles such as 'Beauty Awakes'. He is right, in that none of the pictures in this book carries a title; they all are relatively informal outdoor shots. 'In place of symbolised qualities,' he says, we have 'three professional models doing a job of work and no doubt looking forward to a cup of tea.'

The introduction also tells us that Yvonne Gregory used a large camera, which actually appears in one shot, while her husband used a very small one – presumably 35mm.

Another welcome innovation, compared with books published before this one, is in the layout of pictures on the page. Hitherto most publishers had provided one picture per page, usually slap in the middle. Here we have some variety, with images occasionally two to a page or placed off centre.

There are actually more than the three different models mentioned by Mr Warwick, who are shot in locations that vary between countryside, swimming pool, seashore, and onboard boats. Nearly all the photographs were taken in sunshine. Despite the relative informality of the images, the poses are almost universally graceful.

The book appears to have been printed in photogravure, and is a rather fine example of a style of photography which has now been overtaken by time.

✦ Morning, Noon, Night

Schaeffer, Samuel Bernard,
New York: Knight

Not seen, but said to be 12¼" x 9½". This was an American publication but was advertised for sale in the UK, by mail order, in *Health and Efficiency* in 1939. I suspect that very few copies were ever sold here.

The book was apparently an arty piece of work containing a number of nude figure studies by Schaeffer. The photographs follow a family throughout the day, as they go about their activities in the home, unclothed. Very odd. There are also '15 adaptations from the photographs by well respected commercial artists of the time.' Spiral binding, but the original edition seems to have been sold in a box, so it was probably expensive.

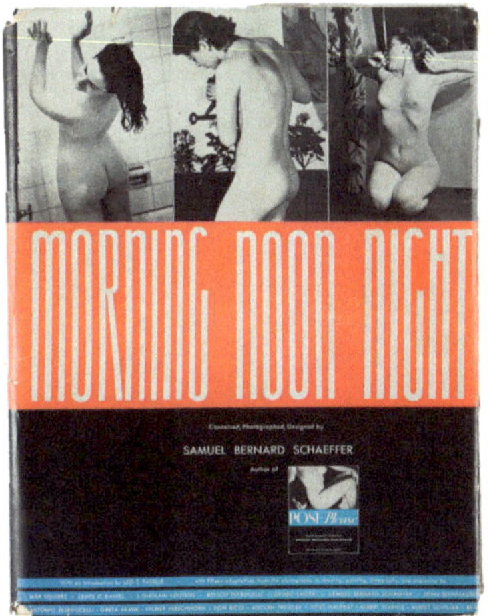

✦ Living Sculpture – Curves and Contrasts of the Human Figure

Sunbathing Society of Bristol and the Clarendon Press, Size 9¾" x 7"

This is an oddity. It is a hardback book but the spine offers no title; also, there are no names of photographers or other contributors given anywhere. The title page states that the book is published by the Sunbathing Society of Bristol, England, and the copyright page claims 'world copyright' for the Clarendon Press, London and New York.

The book is not, as far as I know, listed in any standard bibliography or database; I have only once seen it listed in a bookseller's catalogue, when I bought it.

The title is a combination of Park and Gregory's 1926 and 1936 publications. The learned introduction is in places identical to that by G.M. Ellwood in the 1926 book, but is here uncredited. The pictures are mostly identical to those in the 1936 book, but the printing is of much inferior quality. My copy of the book dates from 1940, and is the tenth reprint. Like quite a few wartime publications of nudes, this one no doubt sold well and provided many a happy hour's entertainment for servicemen far from home.

What was going on? Were Park and Gregory for some reason allowing their work to be used anonymously by the Sunbathing Society of Bristol, perhaps to raise funds? Or was the Society non-existent and the whole thing a rip-off? Given that Park and Gregory were evidently supporters of the sunbathing/nudist movement, I suspect the former.

✦ Beauty's Daughters

Bird, Walter,
John Long, Size 12½" x 10"

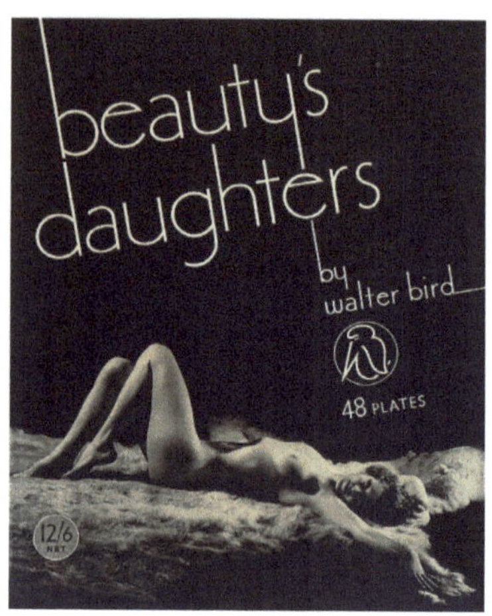

The dust jacket features an abandoned nude lying invitingly on a bearskin rug – really quite a daring image. The flyleaf identifies the lady as Miss Mathea Merryfield. It seems likely that she was a cabaret artist of the time; certainly Bird often used showgirls as his models. The publisher's blurb goes on to say that 'here, captured for the delight of the eye, is the beauty, so often fleeting, of the female form.' Which is refreshingly frank and straightforward.

The introduction is by Fortunio Matania, who maintains that Walter Bird 'is guided only by principles of art'. As opposed to principles of commerce, presumably. Matania then goes on to claim that the position of women who pose for artists and photographers has recently undergone a change. Now, he asserts, women can pose nude without damage to their moral reputations, but it is the artists who are now reluctant to portray them! This, he argues, is an incomprehensible phenomenon. And if photographers are now prepared to step in where artists fear to tread, so much the better for everyone.

The 48 plates which follow are printed on one side of the paper only, one image to a page; the pictures usually fill almost all the space, with a black border of 1/8th of an inch. Mr Bird is one of those who give titles to their pictures. In this case the titles are fairly predictable to anyone familiar with the genre: Meditation, Devil Dance, etc.

The images themselves are often quite striking. Nearly all were taken in the studio, though there are half a dozen outdoor shots at the end. The model is often caught as if in the middle of a dance, and perhaps that's exactly what she was doing. Props are frequently in evidence, and are sometimes fairly elaborate. The lighting effects are almost invariably low key.

The cover girl, Mathea Merryfield, is again identified as one of the models, and there are several shots of Rosemary Andrée.

All in all, this is a book which demonstrates that Walter Bird took his art rather seriously and was pretty good at it. He was a close colleague of John Everard and Roye, who at around this time were sharing studio facilities together; and, as we shall see, they later published together.

When I first came to write this description, I could not immediately find my copy of the book, and assumed that I had been mistaken in thinking that I had one. So I did an internet search to see if I could buy a copy. And indeed there was one: available from a Dutch bookseller at a mere £191.

✦ Perfect Womanhood

Roye (pseudonym for Horace Roye-Narbeth),
Routledge, Size 10" x 7½"

Yet another in the 'Seen by the Camera' series. This is Roye's first appearance in hardback.
He was a formidable talent and an impressive personality; I shall say a little more about his
life when we come to his autobiography, published in 1955.

Not surprisingly, given the no-nonsense nature of the man, this book makes no pretence
of being a collection of studies for art students or anything of that ilk. The flyleaf states
plainly that the collection 'displays the female form in a striking and attractive manner'.
And that's that.

There is an introduction, in the form of a letter from someone who signs himself Raymond. The letter is addressed to Diana, who is evidently his niece or daughter. It briefly
outlines Roye's career to date and declares that he is 'a genius with a camera'. Well, he
was certainly very talented. In these photographs, Raymond tells Diana that she will find
'ease, assurance and carefree laughter – women who are unashamed and confident in their
beauty'. Which is not a bad description of the images which follow.

As usual, there are 48 pages of plates, all of them outdoor shots of one or two models.
Many of these photographs were reproduced in magazines and books over and over again
in the years that followed. Roye was perhaps the most skilful of all the photographers listed
in this bibliography at getting the maximum commercial mileage out of his work. But then
it was outstandingly good.

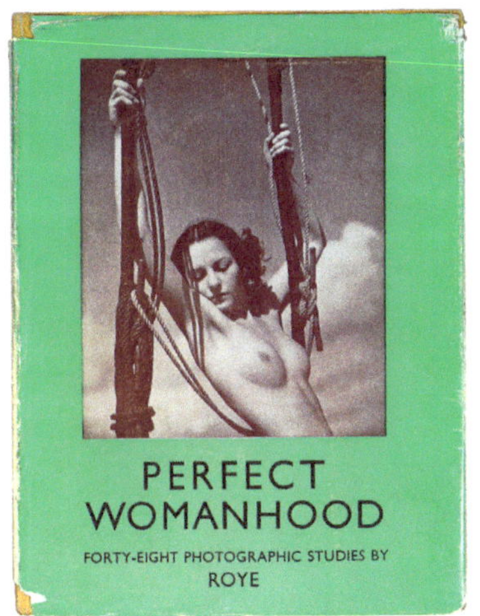

✦ Photography of the Figure in Colour and Monochrome

Simpson, Charles Walter,
H.F. & G. Witherby, Size 9" x 6"

This is another bibliographic puzzle. The COPAC entries maintain that the publisher is
Witherby, as stated above. However, the copy of the book which I own tells a different
story. On the dust jacket the spine gives the publisher as American Photography, and the
price as $5.00. The flyleaf gives the publisher as the American Photographic Publishing
Company, of Boston, Massachusetts.

The title page repeats those data, though the word 'colour' is given the English spelling,
and yet the reverse of the title page states that the book was made and printed in Great
Britain. So what was going on here? Well, maybe the book really was originally published
in England, and what I have is a version prepared specially for the American market. In my
copy, plates 8 and 9 do not appear, but plates 10 and 11 appear twice.

Be that as it may, the book consists mainly of text (201 pages), with 103 plates interspersed. The term 'figure' is interpreted to mean the human body both clothed and unclothed, and indeed it is mainly clothed. Of the pictures which are nudes, Simpson himself provides only a handful; the others are provided by John Everard and one or two others. Although the book is now very dated, Simpson still has one or two interesting things to say.

✦ Portrait of a Model

Everard, John,
Routledge, Size 12½" x 10¼"

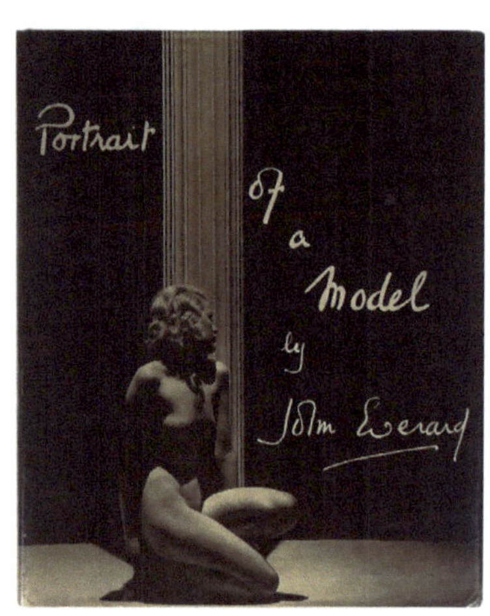

A large and very handsomely produced volume, with an introduction by Charles Simpson, whose own book is discussed above.

The introduction sings the praises of Mr Everard, without being too pompous and trying our patience too severely, but Mr Simpson does not really tell us anything that we couldn't have worked out for ourselves.

The photographs – 48 of them, as usual – are printed on one side of the paper only, and the paper is unusually heavy. The print quality is excellent. The same model is used throughout, and this, I am sorry to say, results in a certain monotony. The model is not named. Mostly studio shots, with a handful taken out of doors.

On the whole I am inclined to think that this is John Everard's least successful book.

✦ A Study of Sunlight and Shadow on the Female Form

Park, Bertram, Gregory, Yvonne,
John Lane, Size 11" x 8"

Subtitled 'for artists and art students', the flyleaf of this book tells us that it is 'primarily intended for the artist and student', but that 'it must also appeal to all lovers of the beautiful in nature and in woman'.

There is an introduction by Bernard Adams, who discusses the relationship between photography and art. He mentions that in London's Tate Modern there is (or was) a portrait of Gwen Ffrangcon Davies by Richard Sickert on whose canvas the artist has written 'painted from a photograph by Bertram Park.'

What can we make of this? To me it suggests that the publishers had found themselves the subject of some criticism for selling collections of nude photographs, and, in time-honoured fashion, were covering their arses with talk of artists and students. We shall encounter yet more of this in the years that follow.

There are 63 pages of photographs, all of them excellent and well printed. The large majority are outdoor shots, sometimes with as many as three models in view. This is one of my favourite books from the period. The original price was 8s. 6d. In 1963 I bought a copy in Tunbridge Wells for 2s. 6d. That copy went missing somewhere along the line, and the next time I bought one, in 1985, it cost me £10. On the day that I write this, there is one for sale online at £45, which strikes me as good value.

✦ The English Maid

Roye,
Routledge, Size 10" x 7½"

Part of the 'Seen by the Camera' series. The flyleaf tells us that this is the first in a planned sequence of books by Roye, which will eventually cover maids from Wales, Ireland and Scotland, as well as England.

There is a foreword, unsigned. As with Roye's previous book, this records his substantial achievements as a photographer, and the public recognition accorded to him to date. The foreword remarks, too, upon the spontaneity and naturalness of Roye's models. And this, surely, is the key to Roye's work. Technically he was very skilful, but a more important factor was his ability to get his models to relax and look happy. Whether he was on physically intimate terms with any or all of them I don't know, and I don't much care, but when looking at these pictures one senses a lack of inhibition in the model which contributes greatly to a successful image.

Nobody should be under any illusion that a good working relationship between model and photographer is easy to achieve. In his 1937 book *The Model* (discussed above) Mortensen points out that the inexperienced photographer is often embarrassed and surprised to find how unmanageable an apparently cooperative model can be! He goes on to devote many pages to advising photographers on how to achieve their desired effects. But in the end, of course, it is all a matter of personality, and Roye had what it takes.

All 48 shots are of single models, and all were taken out of doors. The quality of the printing is crisp and clean. One of the most famous of these photographs (page 10) was exhibited in the London Salon of Photography in 1938, under the title 'Sport'. It was promptly reproduced in the *Daily Mirror* on 14 September 1938, thus becoming (according to Roye) the first nude study ever printed in a British national newspaper. The model was Strelsa Brown, and she was 6' 1" tall.

✦ Nymph and Naiad

Everard, John,
Routledge, Size 12½" x 10"

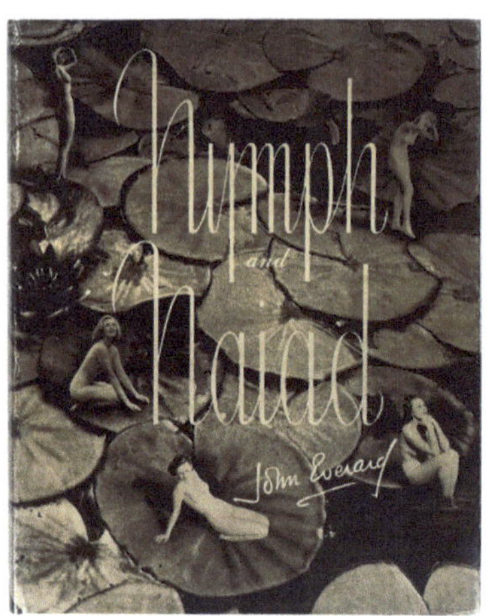

An altogether bigger and more expensive book than Routledge's 'Seen by the Camera' series, which at this time were retailing at 4s. This book cost 15s. and closely resembles *Portrait of a Model*. In retrospect, it seems a strange book for a publisher to have brought out in wartime, but perhaps planning was well advanced before war was declared.

The dust jacket is a highly elaborate montage of miniature nude water nymphs besporting themselves on top of water lilies. The short introduction is by the photographer himself. He declares that, although this is his fifth book of nudes, he is only just beginning to find himself and to know what he is doing.

Mr Everard seems once again to have used only one model, who is again unnamed. There are 48 plates, printed on one side of the paper only, as with *Portrait of a Model*. The majority of the shots were taken out of doors, in the summer of 1939, and, of these, most were taken with a 35 mm camera.

The pictures themselves are excellent, and beautifully printed. In many of them, Mr Everard makes heavy use of backlighting effects.

Blonde and Brunette

'Jason' (obviously a pseudonym; real name unknown),
Chapman and Hall, Size 10" x 7½"

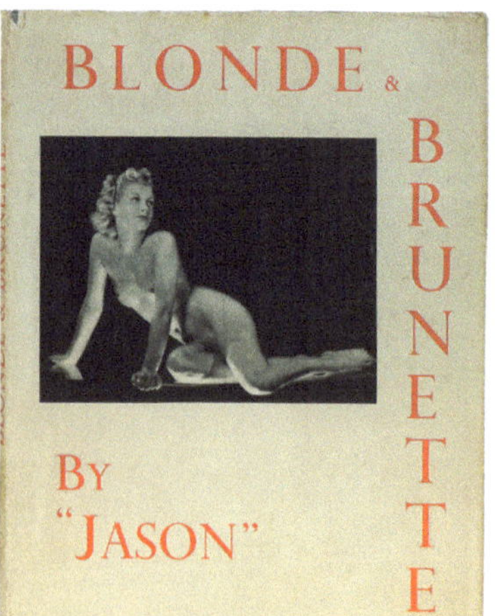

The name Jason is placed in inverted commas on the spine and on the title page of the book. There is a brief author's note, saying that the 32 nude studies here presented are his first attempt at such work. He thanks his models, Margaret, Valerie, and Desirée, and also thanks the owner of Soho's Windmill Theatre for allowing the girls to have time off to pose. Desirée went on to pose for Roye, who gave her a book of her own (published in 1942).

The photographs are all taken in the studio and are orthodox in style. They are distinguished mainly by the beauty of the models – but then you would expect no less from Windmill girls.

✦ The Scottish Maid

Roye,
Routledge, Size 10" x 7½"

Number two in Roye's 'Maids' sequence, this is again part of the 'Seen by the Camera' series and is identical in format with the rest of them. It has the usual 48 plates.

There is a foreword, unsigned, which maintains that there are three types of feminine beauty in North Britain: the fair Anglo-Saxon type of the Lowlands, the dark Celtic type of the Highlands, and the Scandinavian type from the Orkneys and Shetlands. Well, maybe. But personally I would not bet any substantial amount of money that any of these models actually came from anywhere north of Watford. To my eye they look much the same – and just as delightful – as the English maids who preceded them and the Welsh and Irish maids who would follow.

None of which is to underrate Roye's achievement. His 48 images were all taken out of doors, and all are first class. It is noticeable that, even here, he was beginning to lose patience with the law about pubic hair. In several of these images there is only a perfunctory attempt to airbrush out the offending substance, and I imagine that the extent to which this was done was debated at some length between photographer and publisher. Given that London was then in the middle of the Blitz, Roye can be forgiven for thinking that Londoners had more important things to worry about.

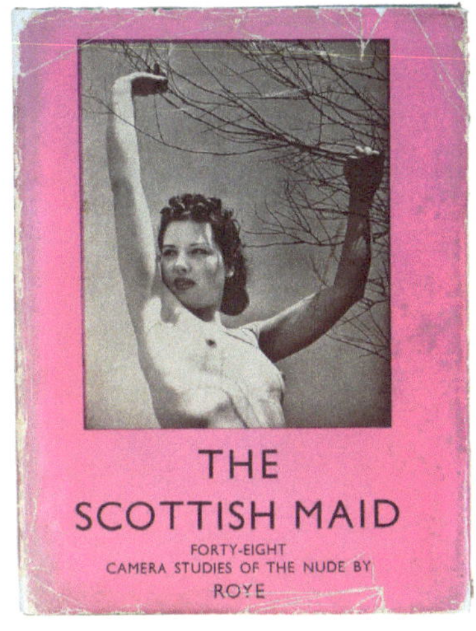

1941

✦ Beauty's Self

Bird, Walter,
John Long, Size 10" x 7½"

This is a much smaller and less expensively produced book than Walter Bird's first effort (*Beauty's Daughters*, 1938). The cheaper format may have resulted from wartime economies, or it may have been an attempt to reach a different market.

The foreword – which consists of one paragraph – maintains that the book *Beauty's Daughters* 'illustrated the beauty which could be obtained by the play of light upon a figure, the result being of more import than the beauty of the body itself'. (Oh, yeah?) For the present book, however, 'the ideal in view was the portrayal of the beauty of women'; in other words, the purpose of the book is just to show us some exceptionally good-looking women – a purpose to which no one could have any reasonable objection. The photographer, says the foreword, has aimed at 'spontaneous simplicity', whatever that is. (There must be a special school somewhere that these blurb writers go to.)

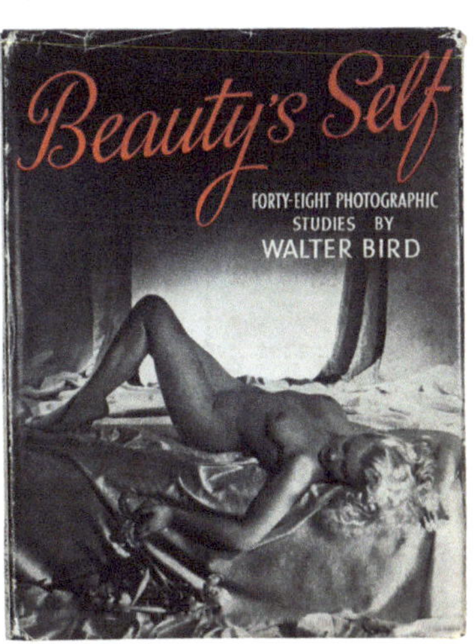

There follow the usual 48 plates. Each image was shot in the studio, and they are all exceptionally well lit. Bird certainly knew what he was doing. He also chose models with good figures: at least one of them was used by Jason in his 1940 book, so the Windmill Theatre may have been the source.

In his autobiography (see 1955), Roye tells us that Bird was troubled by two impersonators. One would ring up the Windmill, pretending to be Walter Bird, and ask to speak to one of the showgirls. He would then subject her to obscene abuse. The other impersonator was even cheekier: he persuaded at least one girl to audition for him in the nude, and, with the aid of a razor, proceeded to make her 'more suitable for nude photography'. The girl's mother eventually smelt a rat. The police, Roye tells us, tried hard to trace these enterprising fellows, but they were unable to make arrests.

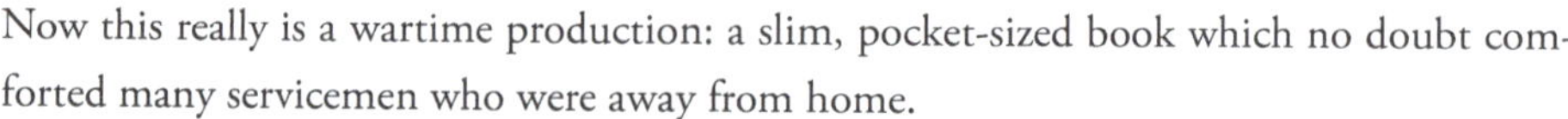

✦ Eves without Leaves

Bird, Walter, Everard, John, and Roye,
Pearson, Size 7¼" x 5¼"

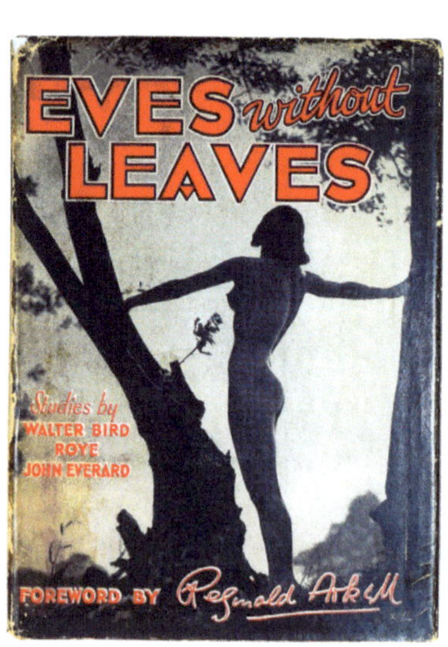

Now this really is a wartime production: a slim, pocket-sized book which no doubt comforted many servicemen who were away from home.

As early as 1939, Bird, Everard, and Roye had decided that they were giving each other too much competition. To resolve that difficulty, they decided to cooperate, and they set up a company called Photo Centre Ltd. They made their headquarters in a suite of rooms above Walter Bird's studio in Savile Row, and *Eves without Leaves* was their first joint publication.

Most if not all of the images are taken from the three photographers' previous books, and all of them had also been published in the magazine *Men Only*. The editor of that journal supplies a foreword, which is a decidedly tongue-in-cheek piece. He claims that the number of nude studies in his magazine has been strictly limited, and that he personally would have been much happier if the publisher of the present book had stuck to pictures of village churches and thatched cottages. But at least we are spared all the twaddle about 'spontaneous simplicity' and the like.

All of the photographs (47 of them) are given titles, even if they did not have them in their previous publications. Roye, of course, demonstrates his contempt for that sort of phoney classicism by entitling one of his pictures 'Bank Holiday at Brighton'. It shows a naked girl heaving on two ropes, as if pulling a boat out of the water.

There are frequent references to our heroes' other books, which were no doubt still in print, and at the end there are details of how to obtain prints at the specially reduced price of 2s. 9d. each; the normal price it is said, would be 10s. 6d. The driving force behind this commercialism was undoubtedly Roye, as his autobiography (see 1955) makes clear.

✦ More Eves without Leaves

Bird, Walter, Everard, John, and Roye,
Camera Studies Club, Size 7¼" x 5"

The Pearson publication by England's three leading photographers of the nude (listed left) was undoubtedly a success, and Roye for one realised that there was money to be made in a sequel.

The Camera Studies Club, which acted as publisher for this book, was a Roye enterprise. In his autobiography (see 1955) Roye tells us that he invited Everard and Bird to be his partners in setting up the Club, but they declined, seeing little chance of profit in it. Which only goes to show that Roye was a great deal more astute in financial matters than they were. Undaunted, he simply agreed with them a price for the use of their photographs, and ran the Camera Studies Club on his own. There is no doubt that Roye made a great deal of money out of this and several other companies that he set up.

The 32 photographs in *More Eves without Leaves* follow the same pattern as the original. They are mostly extracted from previously published books, which are given a plug under the relevant picture. The models are for the most part exceptionally beautiful and are photographed to the highest professional standards, resulting in a series of striking and memorable images.

At the end the reader is again offered the opportunity to purchase prints, this time for 3s. 3d. each. The price had gone up since the first book – but then it was wartime. There are also advertisements for other books by Roye, Everard, and Bird, all of which were, of course, available from the Camera Studies Club.

And, what is more, there are adverts for smaller, paperback publications, the *Spotlight on Beauty* series. (Because they were paperback and were more in the nature of booklets or one-off magazines, these publications are not listed in this bibliography.) The *Spotlight on Beauty* booklets were the forerunners of the pocket-sized 32- or 48-page publications which in the 1950s and '60s would be widely sold through newsagents. Yes indeed, Roye was no sort of slouch when it came to commerce.

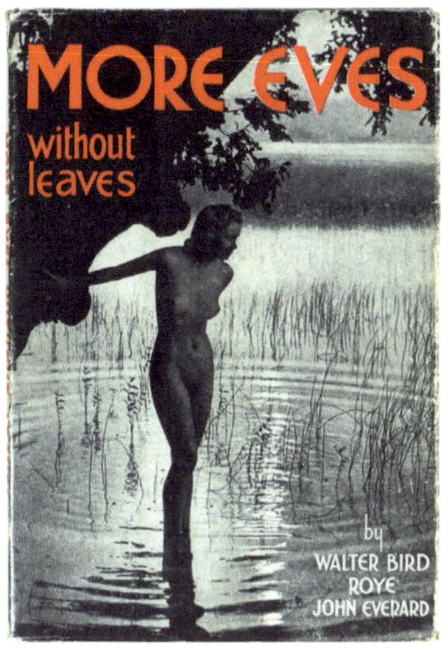

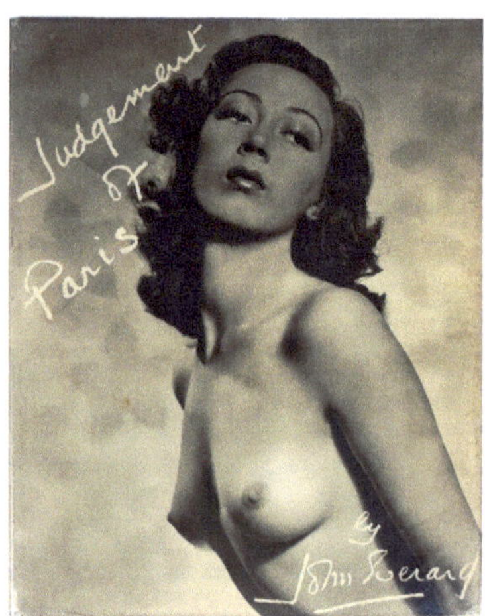

✦ The Judgement of Paris

Everard, John,
Routledge, Size 12½" x 10"

Yet another large and handsomely produced volume from Routledge. Once again I have to say that it seems odd, in retrospect, that it should have been possible to produce such an expensive book as this in wartime. However, there was no doubt an argument that life had to go on.

The title page tells us that there is an introduction by the author, but the heading of the text reads Preface. The first thing that we are told is that Mr Everard actually travelled to Paris to create this book, and that the Germans were knocking at the northern gates of the city when he left by the southern route! So presumably he was there in the spring of 1940. Models, he says, were hard to come by, because all the cabarets were closed. When he did find suitable girls (he insisted that they should actually be French, and not just working in Paris), he found that they invariably turned up two hours late. You see, you just can't get the staff any longer…

Mr Everard's troubles were not over. There was a censor to be dealt with – a Colonel de Massignac, no less. However, on seeing copies of the photographer's previous books the Colonel generously gave permission for the latest batch of images to be exported from the city. Apparently, the Parisians normally like to keep such pictures to themselves. Well, there you go. It's a hard life being a photographer of nudes.

In conclusion, John Everard tells us that he has now published, in book form, 268 photographs; this is, he says, 220 more than he ever expected to publish. After all that, what of the plates? Well, there are 48 of them, as usual, immaculately printed studio shots, on one side of the paper only, with a blank reverse. Many of the shots are low key. The fashion for young Parisian women in that year seems to have been to shave off your eyebrows and paint in a thin straight pencil line instead. Shaving pubic hair, however, does not seem to have been in fashion, and by the look of it the retoucher had a few problems.

These photographs by Everard are skilful, classical, and professional, but they are perhaps lacking in that tension or understanding between photographer and model which Roye and some others could provide.

✦ Arthur Ferrier's Lovelies Brought to Life by Roye

Ferrier, Arthur, and Roye,
Chapman and Hall, Size 9¾" x 6¾"

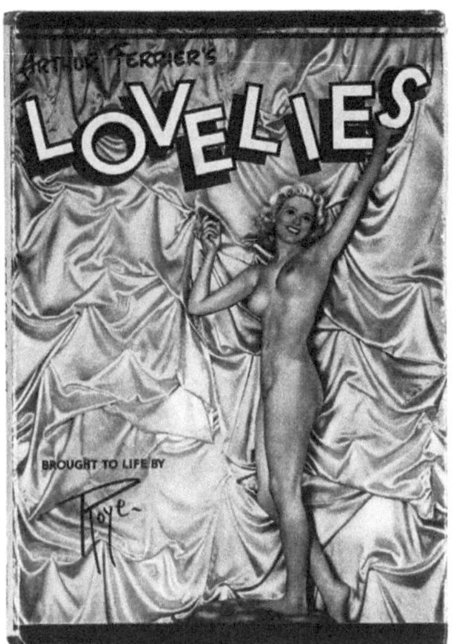

This is a curiosity. Arthur Ferrier was a cartoonist, or perhaps illustrator would be a better word. He specialised in drawing pinup girls. Roye, of course, was Roye. The basic idea behind this book was evidently for Roye to take a number of Ferrier's drawings of glamorous young ladies, and then to photograph models, in the nude, in the same sort of pose or state of mind. An odd starting point, but no doubt one which was thought to be promising from a commercial point view. As a piece of light-hearted fun it succeeds admirably, which is just as well because in 1941 the men of the nation were seriously in need of something to brighten their day.

There is a publishers' foreword, which is admirably down to earth and much less stuffy than most of these things. The publishers explain that, when they first heard about the idea for the book, they were sceptical; Roye's part in the proceedings would, they thought, be particularly difficult. They point out that, traditionally, to publish a picture of a smiling nude has been 'to invite the onslaught of all the prudes of the Purity League'. But Roye, they believe, has achieved his purpose admirably, and without impropriety. They point out, incidentally, that the photographs in this book are the first studio shots of nudes that Roye has ever published, all his previous work having been taken out of doors.

The publishers invite us to note that there are four models featured, all of whom have been in theatrical productions mounted by George Black – and all of whom, I am pretty sure, had featured in Roye's previous books.

Each girl is shown in eight plates, which are printed on one side of the paper only. The nudes are shown on the top right of each page, with Ferrier's pen and ink ladies on the left and sometimes below. The link between drawing and photograph is sometimes a bit tenuous, but hey – let us not look a gift horse in the mouth.

✦ The Feminine Figure

Gotlop, Philip,
Thorsons, Size 11¼" x 8¼"

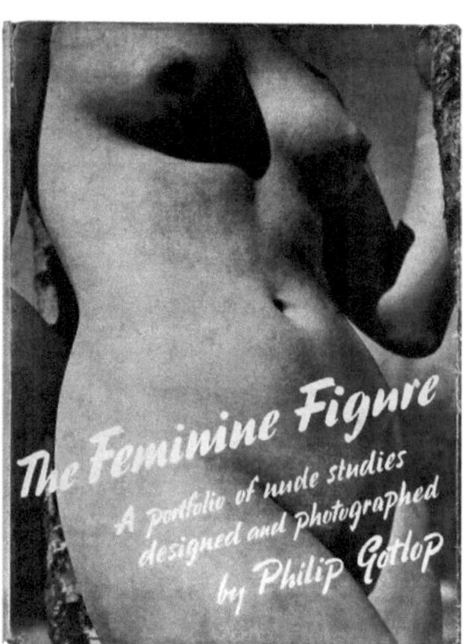

Not only photographed but also designed by Philip Gotlop, says the title page. There is an introduction by William Welby, who was a well-known writer on nudism (*Naked and Unashamed*, *It's Only Natural*, etc). He says that he has found it difficult to secure illustrations for his books on nudism because the majority of professional photographers seem to be obsessed with the 'Art Plate' idea of nude photography. He argues that nude photography should ideally feature realism and movement, because 'beauty is at its highest when in action'. He adds that this book is Gotlop's first effort in the field, so *Eve Unveiled* (see entry below) was presumably published second.

There is then an author's preface, confirming that, as far as possible, each pose exemplifies action, either in movement, design, or expression. Gotlop goes on to provide a certain amount of technical information about cameras, lenses and so forth, and encourages the amateur photographer to 'go to it'.

The book features three models, all of whom have good figures and very 1940s hairstyles, and are all pictured out of doors. The posing is fairly uninspired. There are 93 plates in total. This was no doubt a pretty exciting book in its day, but it is chiefly of historical interest now.

✦ Eve Unveiled

Gotlop, Philip,
Jarrolds, Size 10" x 7½"

Gotlop's second book of the year. The inside flap of the dust jacket tells us that the 48 shots of the five models were all taken out of doors in the month of April. Each study has been 'carefully thought out in order to deviate as far as possible from any set posing'. The photography, claim the publishers, is 'masterly', and 'from a technical point of view the volume should be of great value to students'. Which is drivel, of course, and the photography is in fact rather commonplace and uninspired.

There is no introduction or foreword, and after the title page we plunge straight into the first of the 48 plates. We see immediately that there is indeed an absence of 'set posing'. What we have is a series of reasonably attractive women, photographed mostly in rural surroundings. Some of these ladies are well over 21, and they don't look any too warm.

However, we must remember that there were at this time very few places where men could find pictures of nude women; the emotional impact of pictures such as these was no doubt considerable, despite what now seems to us to be second-rate production values. The chaps were jolly grateful for whatever they could get. The book was priced at 5s., which was steep for the working man. Within a year or two, however, the Yanks would be here, and they had lots of money. I once met a man who had known Philip Gotlop, and Mr Gotlop was apparently of the view that it was US dollars which had financed his pension plan.

◆ The Irish Maid

Roye,
Routledge, Size 10" x 7½"

The third instalment of Roye's survey of UK pulchritude. There is not much to say about
this, because the formula is unchanged. Seven pages of text ('Three tributes to the Irish
maid') are followed by the usual 48 pages of outdoor nudes, printed on both sides of the
paper. Beautiful girls, well photographed: Roye varied the use of his camera angle much
more than most at this time. And some of the images have almost undisguised pubic hair.
His publisher no doubt had one or two twitchy moments.

1942

◆ Venus Through the Lens

Barry, John D. Underwood (known professionally as
Dubarry, and referred to as such on the dust jacket),
Thorsons, Size 12¼" x 9¼"

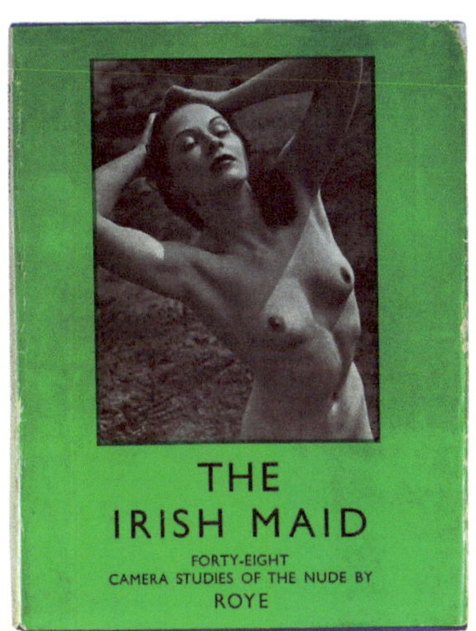

The dust jacket shows a young lady who is chained hand and foot. My word, now there's
a departure. Park and Gregory produced one similar picture ('Despair' in *The Beauty of
the Female Form*) but no photographer, to my knowledge, had previously used a bondage
image on a dust jacket. (Such images were, however, fairly commonplace in nineteenth-
century painting, some of which bordered upon sadomasochistic soft porn.) The rest of the
book, regrettably, is not so daring.

A one-page 'Dramatis Personae' lists the 20 models who posed for Dubarry. Fourteen
of them are named and six remain anonymous. Unusually, the occupation of each – hair-
dresser, civil servant, etc – is given.

Next we have the author's preface, which is more than usually tedious. He begins with
a pompous statement of intent: 'No book has a right to exist which has not for its purpose
the betterment of mankind, by affording either useful information or healthful recreation.'
Dubarry goes on to criticise the 'alleged Art Albums' which are on the market; they feature,
he says, 'stereotyped poses' and 'unnecessary and platitudinous captions'. In them there is
no 'original conception' or 'symbolic design'. Such work is thoroughly bad, of course. The
proper purpose of a book such as this is service: 'It must be serving a portion of humanity
by giving it new inspiration or instruction hitherto inaccessible.'

Fortunately, not everything that Dubarry has to say is nonsense. He does make the
point that an expensive camera does not necessarily produce a good picture, and that cheap
equipment, properly used, is perfectly adequate for the job. He prefers, he says, new and
inexperienced models, because the longer a model has been at work the more likely it is

that she will rely on a number of set and stale poses. And, what's more, the man is not entirely without a sense of humour. In discussing the virtues of blondes as compared with brunettes, he points out that these days a young lady may very well turn out to be both. The remainder of the (fairly long) preface provides technical information on developers, etc, which has long since become out of date.

There follow 70 separate photographs, some of them two to a page, and not very well printed. In each case the photographer gives an approximate idea of the lighting used. Despite all the talk about lack of originality in the work of other photographers, these images seem to me to be absolutely orthodox studio shots without any great inspiration behind them. Almost all are taken from the same head-on camera position. One or two of the models are mature ladies, which is welcome, but otherwise there is not much to excite the eye.

✦ Eve

Peacock, Anthony (pseudonym for Anthony Peacock Pochin),
Link House, Size 11½" x 10"

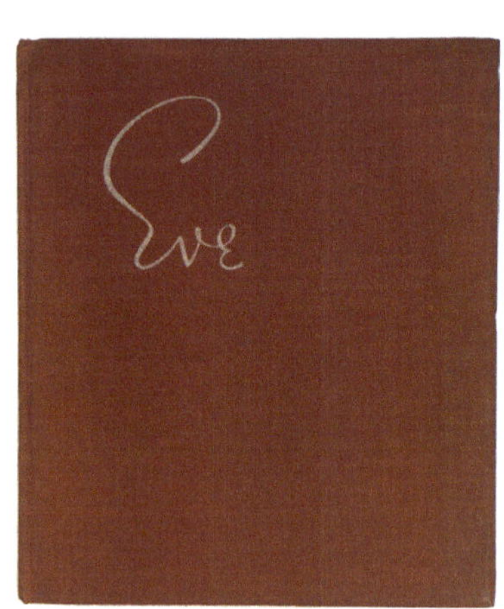

The dust jacket is most discreet: just the one-word title and a silhouetted female figure. A publisher's note contents itself with claiming that 'Antony Peacock is a worthy interpreter of the female form divine,' which is fair enough.

There is then a foreword by D.G. Johnson, the editor of *Health and Efficiency*. He commends the photographer for his straightforward approach, and welcomes the fact that many of the photographs were taken in naturist camps. Peacock apparently sought to simplify the art of nude photography, using one camera, one film, one developer, and a minimum of accessories and props.

It is not surprising that the editor of *Health and Efficiency* should have been called in to say his piece, because Peacock wrote a regular column for the magazine at about this time. Usually he commented on nude studies sent in by readers. He often had sensible things to say about how the model should be posed to good effect, and he was probably influential in this respect. His own ideas seem to have been derived from Mortensen.

There are 66 images in all, one to a page. The majority are outdoor shots, but the collection begins and ends in the studio. The studio shots are mostly high key, with plain white backgrounds. All the images are well printed, with good contrast, and the models are gracefully posed. On this evidence, Peacock was able to practise as well as preach.

✦ Desirée

Roye,
Chapman and Hall, Size 10½" x 8½"

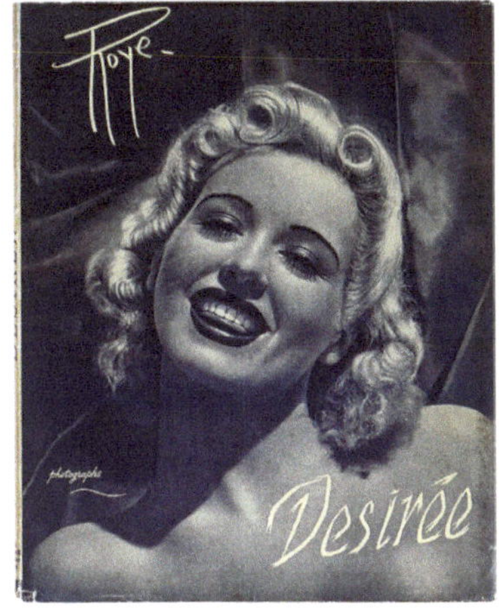

Pedants should note that the name Desirée is printed without an acute accent over the first e on the title page and on the spine of the book, but with an accent on the front cover of the book.

There are 32 plates, each of them featuring the showgirl whose name really was Desirée Cooper; she was a New Zealander. In his autobiography (see 1955), Roye relates that, during the war, her family home in Kew, London, was bombed and her father was killed, but Desirée herself escaped unharmed. After Roye's death, the *Amateur Photographer* published a slightly different version of the story: in that account, Desirée was working late for Roye and he persuaded her to stay out in central London, thus perhaps saving her life. Eventually she married an American Brigadier General.

Not all of the images in this book are nude shots. We begin with eight taken 'in the garden'; then we have eight in the studio, eight in the country, and finally eight by the sea.

This book was a wartime publication, it must be remembered, and the paper used for it is definitely of inferior quality; the reproduction of the images is therefore less than perfect. George Orwell remarked that wartime paper was like lavatory paper, whereas wartime lavatory paper had become like sheet tin. Part of the problem was that, in December 1940, the area around St Paul's Cathedral had been largely burnt to the ground; and it was in these streets that publishers had traditionally been located. In one night, 27 publishers lost their offices and warehouses, and five million books were destroyed.

Roye must have admired Desirée's beauty greatly, because he used some of these shots of her in his groundbreaking *Unique Editions* series (see 1958).

✦ The Welsh Maid

Roye,
Routledge, Size 9¾" x 7¼"

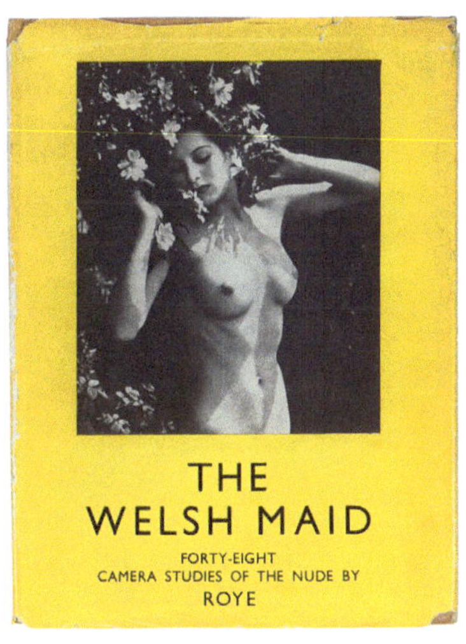

The recipe as before. A brief unsigned foreword, rabbiting on about the beauty of the Welsh. Then 48 pages of images.

Anyone who looks at this book immediately after viewing the other two books of nudes which were published in 1942 will instantly see that Roye was much bolder than the average photographer in his choice of viewpoint. Neither Dubarry nor Peacock seemed capable of taking the camera off its tripod and photographing the model from above, below, or at an angle. But Roye did it much of the time, with the result that his images are that much more striking. As usual, he has stunningly beautiful models who look very much at ease with themselves, and he is well served by his printer. Result: classy material.

✦ Rhapsody in Colour

Roye,
Camera Studies Club, Size 13½" x 11¼"

Spiral bound, with a plastic binder. The Camera Studies Club, run by Roye, was at this time catering for a variety of customers. On the one hand Roye was publishing some pocket-sized booklets containing nudes and pinups, and on the other hand he was producing a positively sumptuous book such as this – for which he no doubt charged a high price. In 1943 the small publications included *Curves and Colour* (3s. 6d.) and Miniature Lovelies (1s. 3d.), both of which contained photographs by Bird, Everard, and Roye. (And, since they were pocket-sized booklets, they will not be further described here.)

Rhapsody in Colour, however, is on an altogether different scale. It contains 12 plates, printed on one side only of the heavy paper; each image is protected by a sheet of tissue paper. All the models are female but not all are nude; the size of the image is usually about 7" x 6". Each picture has a title, printed in a Gothic script, and the protective paper bears a brief verse of relevant poetry. The colour (using the 'new Lifecolour process') is a little garish by our standards, but it must have been striking in its day. A later book by Roye refers to the 'Lifecolour process of Photo Centre Ltd', and Photo Centre was another of Roye's companies, so he may well have had a commercial interest in the printing technology as well as the photographs.

This is, in short, a coffee-table book. Judging by its current availability in the second-hand market, the book must have been sold all over the world. Oddly enough, towards the end of his life Roye did not own a copy, and I was asked to help him obtain one.

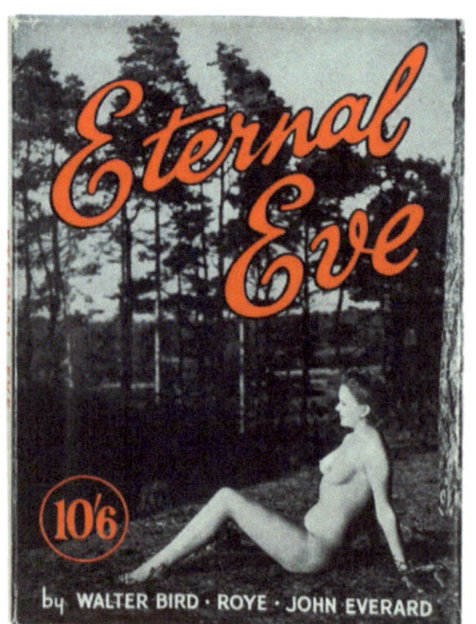

✦ Eternal Eve

Bird, Walter, Everard, John, and Roye,
Elstree, Size 7¼" x 5"

Not seen, but it seems likely that this book is a rehash of the earlier published work of these gentlemen. Roye, in particular, was adept at getting the maximum mileage out of anything. Elstree Publications Ltd was the company which ran the Camera Studies Club. The book contains 32 plates, so presumably was a victim of the post-war paper shortage.

✦ Maids

Roye,
Elstree, Size 9½" x 7¼"

The book contains 32 plates, eight from each of Roye's four previous *Maids* books (*The English Maid*, and so on). A 'publisher's announcement' on the first page tells us that the four books are now out of print and it has not been possible to obtain enough paper to reprint all of them; hence the selection of eight images from each book.

Never slow to exploit a commercial opportunity, Roye published this book through his own company. The quality of the printing is fair to middling, given the circumstances of the time.

1950

✦ The Technique of Nude Photography
Volumes I and II

Gotlop, Philip,
Thorsons, Size 11" x 8"

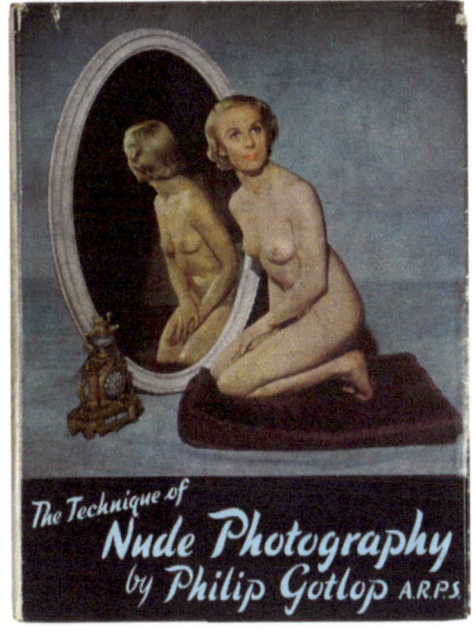

Gotlop is not one of my favourite photographers, but he was industrious, and of course he had to work within the conventions of the time; and it was certainly much easier to publish a collection of nudes under the cover of an instructional manual than it was to present them simply for their own sake. Hence this two-volume treatise.

In the author's preface, Gotlop tells us that he is attempting to pass on what he has learnt: which is a perfectly sensible objective. Volume I contains 51 plates, each printed on the right-hand page. The left-hand page includes numerous technical details of how the shot was taken, together with a lighting plan, details of the lens, etc. The shots feature the usual variety of locations: studio, indoors, outdoors. The models are often those who featured in Gotlop's earlier books. At the end there are half a dozen shots of men.

Volume II is more of the same. Mr Gotlop tells us that 'of particular interest are the studies which have been solarised'. Well, they may be of particular interest to him but they are not very interesting to anyone else. Solarisation is a technique which was, I believe, discovered by Man Ray as a result of a darkroom accident; in nudes, for instance, it has the effect of creating a thick black line around the outline of the figure, and gives the image a sort of silvery tone. At one time the photographic journals were full of instructions for creating this effect. However, I once read a sardonic comment from a gallery owner who asserted that solarisation might be all the rage in some quarters, but he had yet to come across anyone who actually wanted to buy a solarised image.

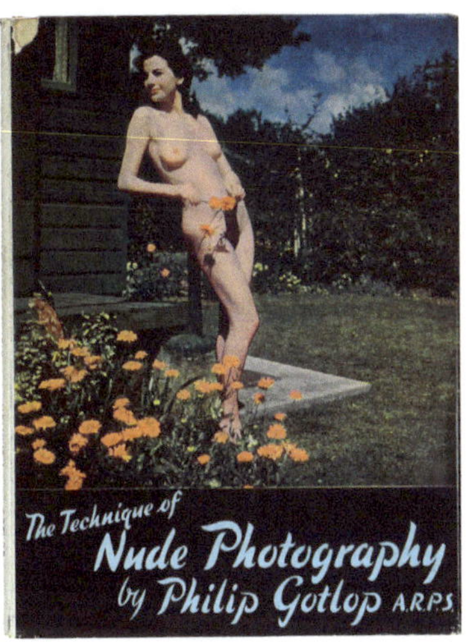

With one or two exceptions, the images in these two volumes seem to me to be rather mundane. In some studio shots, the lighting effects seem crude to my eye; or perhaps they are just badly printed. Either way, they do not appeal. However, this guide to photography of the nude no doubt made Mr Gotlop a large pile of money in its day, so who are we to complain?

1952

✦ Artist's Model

Everard, John,
John Lane, Size 11" x 9"

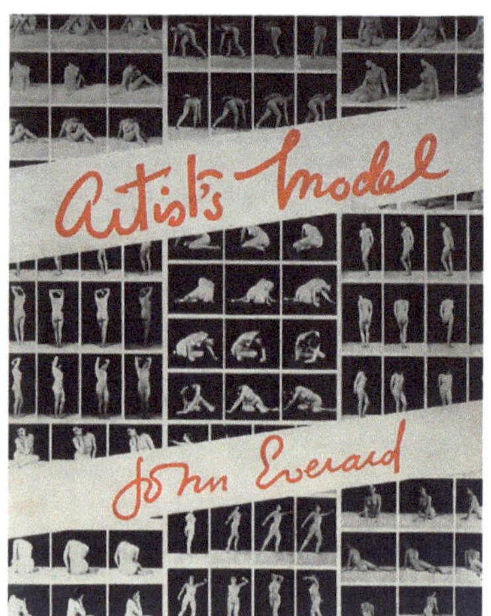

This is the mother and father of all the books which claim to contain 'studies for the student of art.' And for once – just for once – the claim is valid.

The book has been specially designed, says the publisher, 'to become a comprehensive reference work for all artists, sculptors, layout-men and students of the human figure. Over half the book consists of full-page figures each faced by twelve miniature figures of the same pose from different angles.' (These multiple shots of the same pose were achieved by the use of a revolving platform on which the model was placed.)

'There are over a hundred occupational poses showing a woman at her daily tasks from dressing to cleaning.' Oh dear, the feminists aren't going to like that. 'Nearly two hundred fashion poses... Children... Hands... Men in action...' And so on. In short, this is a very different book from the same photographer's *Portrait of a Model* and similar publications. There are over 1,200 photographs in all, 'with an explanatory text of some 15,000 words' written by 'the well-known painter and author Charles Simpson, R.I.'

There is an interesting preface by Everard himself, in which he says that he had realised after the war that 'just another book of nudes' was not going to be acceptable. There had been a spate of such books in the war years, he tells us; some of them had been 'very crude' and lacked 'both artistic and production merit.'

In making this comment, Everard gives us an essential insight into the English psyche of the post-war period. We must remember that in two major wars, England had lost vast numbers of her bravest and best – both men and women. Among those who remained, there arose a widespread desire to pretend that the recent nastiness had never really happened: that the Blitz and Auschwitz had been but horrible dreams. There arose, in short, a desire to put back the clock to an era (which never actually existed) when purity, goodness and truth were the watchwords of every English gentleman.

If you look at the previous few pages of this bibliography, you will see that there were virtually no books containing collections of nudes published between 1943 and this present book of Everard's (apart from the Roye reissues). This is not a coincidence or an omission on the author's part: it is a reflection of a change in the temper of the times.

Book publishers in this era were extremely nervous of offending the authorities through the publication of anything which might be deemed obscene. Across the UK, magistrates seemed to be competing with each other to make fatuous decisions. In 1954, for instance, Swindon magistrates seized copies of Boccaccio's *Decameron*, a literary work which had been famous since the fourteenth century!

And it was not just publishers who were twitchy: the fear of prosecution meant that writers restrained their language, printers refused to print, booksellers and librarians avoided stocking certain books. It was a situation which would not be resolved, and even then not entirely satisfactorily, until the enactment of the Obscene Publications Act of 1959.

In the meantime, John Everard was reduced to producing a book of 'studies for students of art'. And it is an excellent book in its way. Many of the images are fine works in themselves. The majority of the shots were taken in the studio, but some, involving men competing in athletics events and the like, obviously had to be taken in the open air.

Interestingly, there are a number of photographs of naked children which would, as I understand it, be illegal today. A nation which could not possibly allow the word 'fuck' to appear in print was quite unable to cope with the idea that some people might be capable of abusing children.

✦ Figure Photography

Gotlop, Philip,

Jarrolds, Size 11" x 9½"

With 16 anatomical drawings by Alfred Kerr, a professor at 'a noted Chelsea college of art'.

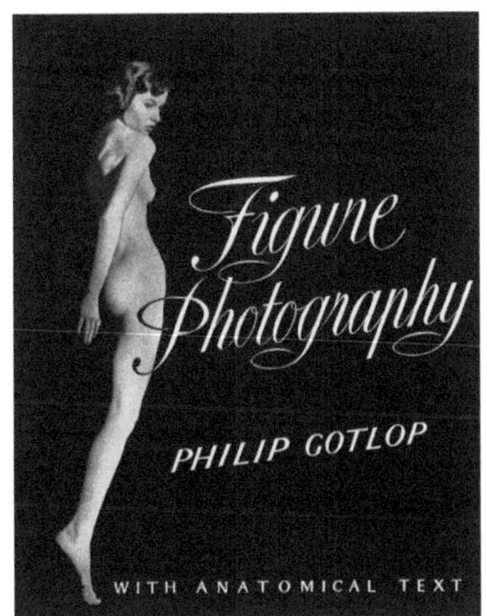

Mr Gotlop and his publishers had got the message too. (See the comments on John Everard's book, above.) The dust jacket of this book announces, on the front, that it comes 'with anatomical text', and the back of the dust jacket bears a complicated diagram of the muscles in a woman's torso. In 1952 it was not sufficient for a book reader to consider a woman beautiful: he had to be taught about her anatomy as well.

And so it wearisomely continues. On the fly leaf, we have the usual claptrap about this being 'a most useful book for artists and sculptors as well as photographers'. Of the 48 plates, the publisher declares tremulously that many of them are 'low key' as it is thought that this is 'the most artistic method' for this type of subject. Abject terror of human sexuality drips out of the book and falls to the floor at the reader's feet.

The photographs are all studio based, and none is particularly inspiring. The anatomical notes were doubtless of zero interest to 999 readers out of a thousand. 'The fullness on the back near the upper arm defines the Teres Major and Minor' we are told. But who cares?

Those criticisms made, it is fair to say that Gotlop's diagrams showing how he lit each shot may well have been useful to some aspiring amateur photographers.

✦ Nudes

Munkacsi, M.,
New York: Greenberg

Not seen, but reported to be 12¾" x 9". Some 76 pages of photographs, which are said to be well printed. There is a foreword by John Rawlings, which does not bode well – see the entry below – but I may be making an unfair judgement.

The BNB says that this book was published in England by Putnam. Judging by booksellers' comments, the 'publishing' process involved nothing more than importing a few copies and sticking a 'Putnam, London' label on to the title page.

✦ 100 Studies of the Figure

Rawlings, John,
Atlas, Size 12" x 10"

Originally published in New York by Studio Publications, an imprint of Thomas Crowell, I believe. I once had a copy of this book but sold it because I found the images so anaemic. If memory serves, Rawlings was a photographer for *Vogue*. In any event, there are 96 pages of 'artistic black and white photographs of one model'. Should you wish to buy a copy of the book, it is easy to find on the secondhand market.

✦ Canadian Beauty

Roye,
Transatlantic Authors for the Camera Studies Club, Size 10¾" x 9"

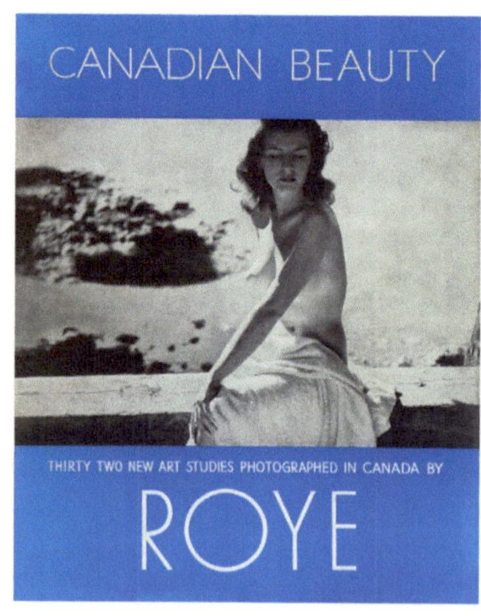

This is Roye once again in self-publishing mode. The book, original price 17s. 6d., contains 32 new 'art studies photographed in Canada'. Two models only are featured, Jannine and Inez, both of whom were beauty contest winners. Inez, the publisher tells us unambiguously, 'is sweet seventeen'. I doubt that a publisher would be so quick to tell us that today. (In some shots, however, Inez looks considerably more mature than seventeen.) In the foreword Roye tells us that the girl was in fact brought to him by her mother.

The photographer provides some interesting comments on technique, making the point that, by varying the combinations of light and shade and camera angle, he has been able to give the impression of using far more than two models – and he is right.

This is not Roye at his very best by any means, but it is a highly professional production. Not all the shots are nudes, and the printing is not exceptional.

✦ My Hundred Best Studies

Everard, John,
John Lane, Size 8¼" x 6½"

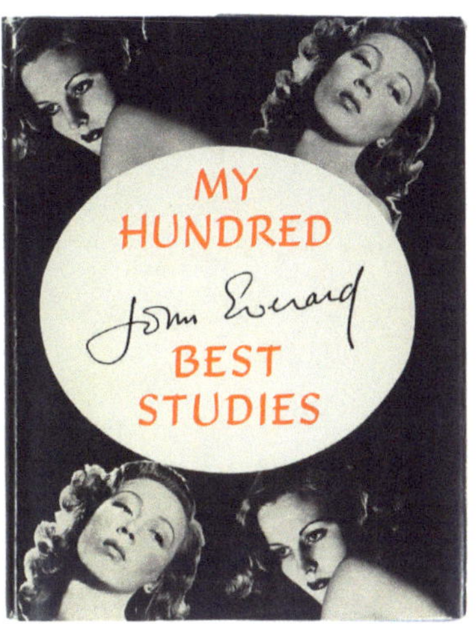

In the preface, Everard tells us that he assembled a selection committee consisting of a sculptor, an artist, a photographer, a medical student, a young woman, an older woman, and 'some others of varying ages and occupations'. This group was asked to look through his previously published work and to select the 'best'.

The remainder of the preface gives us Everard's thoughts on the technique of nude photography, and very interesting they are too. He tells us, for instance, that between 1932 and 1940 he saw approximately 5,000 would-be models!

The plates themselves are excellent. I may, elsewhere in these pages, have been less than wholly enthusiastic about Everard's work, but there is no doubt that he was a major figure. Over a longish period it was almost inevitable that he should have accumulated some beautiful pictures. The images reproduced here are mostly studio work, with a leavening of outdoor shots. If you want just one example of Everard's work, this is the book to buy.

✦ Second Sitting: Another Artist's Model

Everard, John,
John Lane, Size 11"x 8¾"

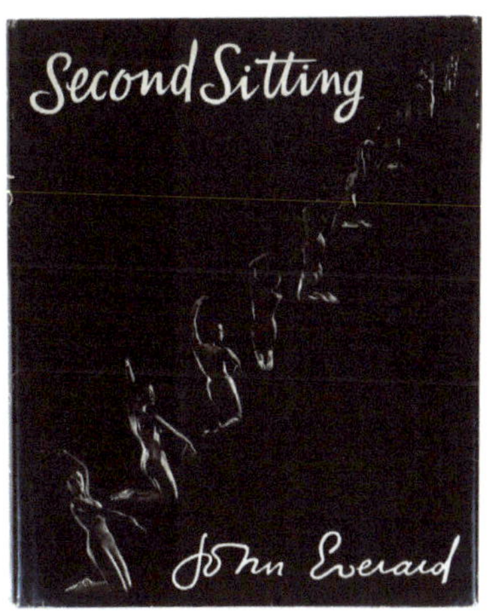

About 170 pages of photographs. Everard's original *Artist's Model* (1952) must have been a commercial success, because now he is back with a sequel. The recipe is much as before, and the images are divided into seven sections: studio studies, female; outdoor studies, female; hand studies, female; child studies; action studies, eyes, and legs; occupational studies; and outdoor studies, male.

Looking through these pages, I have the distinct impression that Everard was becoming more assured in his work; the models look more relaxed. The outdoor studies are particularly pleasing. It is noteworthy, perhaps, that one of the many models featured in this book is a young Pamela Green, who would shortly become famous as the chief model, and partner, of photographer Harrison Marks – of whom more will be said below.

It has to be remembered, however, that we are only in the early 1950s, and prudery still reigns triumphant! When photographing his male models Everard evidently chose to have them pose completely nude; but his publisher must have persuaded him, belatedly, that it was quite impossible to print pictures containing men's dangly bits. As a result, all the men have had a jockstrap painted on to them by an overworked retoucher. This ruins some otherwise rather splendid shots.

✦ How to Shoot for Glamour

Bakal, Carl,

Fountain

Not seen, but said to be 9¾" x 7¾". Originally published in San Francisco by Camera Craft, and probably imported by the Fountain Press. The word 'glamour' in the title had the English spelling, even in the American edition.

It is doubtful whether a 'how to' book properly belongs in this bibliography; and, in addition, 'glamour' is not the same as 'nude'. However, this appears to have been quite a well-produced book, with about 270 photographs by some 40 photographers, including some major names. Among those contributing were Peter Basch, Bernard of Hollywood, and André de Dienes. The cover features Marilyn Monroe in a pink swimsuit.

✦ How to Photograph Women

Gowland, Peter,

Arco

Not seen, but said to be 7" x 5". This is an American book, first published in 1953 by Crown in New York. The Arco 'edition' was probably imported, as usual. The book was later reissued several times, sometimes in a larger size, so it was obviously a good seller. There was also a German edition. The contents are said to include a mixture of nude, bathing-suit and candid shots.

Gowland was certainly a classy photographer, but he was unambiguously commercial rather than 'artistic'.

✦ Oriental Model

Everard, John,

Hale, Size 12½" x 10"

Another handsome coffee-table book, but a new publisher for John Everard. The publisher claims that Everard travelled 40,000 miles while gathering material for this book, including visits to India, Singapore, Japan, and Bali.

The photographer contributes a preface describing his camera and the paper used for prints, etc. And – something which is definitely a first – his wife provides an introduction describing the difficulties that they encountered during their travels! Apparently, it proved to be surprisingly difficult to persuade Eastern ladies to pose in the nude – which does not seem to be the case today

There follows a lengthy Photographic Commentary, possibly by Mrs Everard, with essays on the women of Borneo, the women of Thailand, and so on. The final sentence of the commentary assures us that, 'in spite of rumours to the contrary that ignore the simplest rules of anatomy, there is no fundamental difference in the bodily structure of the Oriental and the Occidental woman.' So that settles that.

There are 48 pages of plates, printed on heavy paper, on one side of the page only, with the picture filling almost all the space. The images are certainly unusual and interesting: one young lady is covered in tattoos and is smoking a cheroot. Heavy retouching of the pubic area is obvious in several shots.

All in all, this is a handsomely produced and intriguing book, one which, in my opinion, is well worth searching for. I cannot imagine, however, how the production of it can have been a cost-effective exercise for Mr Everard. Surely it cannot have sold enough copies to repay him for the time and travel costs involved? Perhaps he had private means.

◆ Nude Ego

Roye,

Hutchinson, Size 9" x 6½"

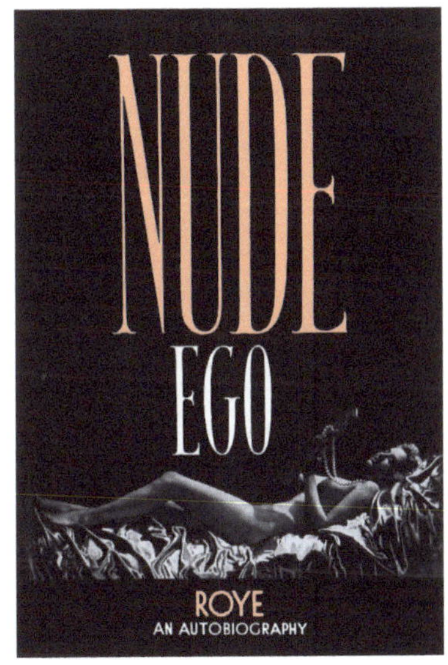

This is Roye's autobiography, and as such it does not, strictly speaking, belong in our list. However, Roye was a major figure in English nude photography, and he was the only photographer of that type to write his life story, so it would be absurd and unhelpful not to mention it. (His full name, incidentally, was Horace Roye-Narbeth.)

The final chapter is perhaps the most important in the book. In it, Roye remarks upon a circumstance which we have already mentioned, namely that in the early 1950s the law of obscenity was being administered in hopelessly inconsistent ways. 'More and more publishers and authors are getting into a tangle with the authorities,' said Roye. 'They are being heavily fined... or let off, according to the personal outlook of the presiding judge and the luck of the draw in juries.' In 1953, for example, four booksellers in Norwich (scarcely a den of vice) had 462 books confiscated, including copies of *Eves Without Leaves* (first published in 1943) and *Desirée* (from 1942).

Roye was quite right, of course, and was wise to be apprehensive about his own position. Before long he would be personally involved in a case which helped to change the law – for details of this, see 1958 and 1960.

Perhaps this is the place to record that, for whatever reason, Roye left England towards the end of the 1950s and seems to have lived abroad thereafter. He made his final home in Rabat, Morocco, where he went water-skiing daily until he was 78; he was to be seen swimming in the river when well into his nineties.

Roye lived to a great age, 96, and had an exhibition of his work in Brighton shortly before his death. He visited the exhibition with his latest girlfriend, who was some sixty years younger than himself. Sadly, he did not die peacefully in bed: in 2002 he was stabbed to death by an intruder at his home in Rabat.

✦ The Nude

de Dienes, André,
John Lane, Size 11" x 8¾"

This is almost the first mention of André de Dienes within these pages, but it will not be the last. He was an exceptionally talented photographer. That judgement is, I think, confirmed by the fact that he was one of the few American photographers to be given a special edition by a UK publisher. Previously, any American photographer who is listed in these pages is usually there simply because a British firm imported a few copies from the States.

The Nude has a foreword by the editor of *Photography*, Norman Hall, who rightly sings de Dienes's praises. He also refers, bravely, to 'the wholesome sensuality of the subject'. In the mid-1950s, as we have seen, few commentators were prepared to admit that the nude had anything to do with sensuality.

There is then a preface by de Dienes himself, in which he reveals that he was born in Hungary, going to the USA only at the age of 25. And it is not unreasonable, perhaps, to see his origins as providing the key to his success in this particular field: he at least was not infected from birth with English or American prudery. De Dienes very sensibly makes the point that he does not fuss about cameras, or even the exposure. A camera, he says, is just a tool, and the type of camera used is of negligible importance. All his photographs are taken with natural light.

The plates take up 100 pages and are divided into five sections: indoors; out of doors; on the terrace; on the sea shore; and composite pictures. Almost without exception they are absolutely first class. By whatever means, de Dienes managed to find exceptionally voluptuous models, and clearly had sufficient rapport with them to get them to pose uninhibitedly. Since he is reported to have had an affair with Marilyn Monroe, we can assume that he had a way with women.

Whether because of the lighting or the printing, or a combination of both, the images have a markedly sculptural quality, something that is noted by Norman Hall in the foreword. Although de Dienes tells us that he did not bother too much about the exposure of each shot, he managed to avoid the burnt-out highlights on the skin which are so commonly seen in many magazine prints of this period.

Just by way of a reminder, perhaps it is worth mentioning that, in all the shots in this book, the pubic area is either hidden, covered by shadow, or has received attention from the retoucher. We are still in the dark ages.

✦ Sculptor's Model: a Third Sitting

Everard, John,
John Lane, Size 11" x 8¾"

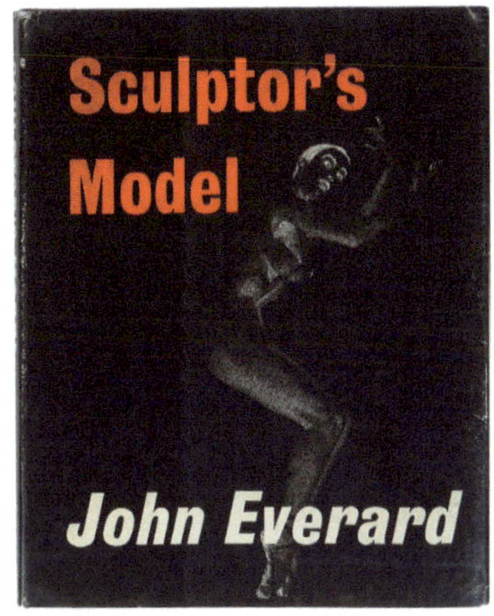

As its title suggests, this volume is very similar to the same photographer's earlier works, *Artist's Model* and *Second Sitting*. There is a preface by the photographer, in which he describes some of the correspondence arising from his previous books. He also tells us that, in planning this book, he had intended to include several mixed groups, i.e. men and women, or men, women and children. However, having produced about 20 pages of such studies, he was advised 'that they would not pass the censor'. Of course there was no censor in a formal sense, but, as we have already noted, all photographers (and writers) were entirely at the mercy of some very odd decisions handed down by magistrates. Everard therefore abandoned his plans to provide images of mixed groups.

'I am constantly baffled,' he says, 'by the difference in people's interpretation of what is decent.' And he points out that several Latin countries consider the shaved model to be highly 'exposed' and therefore offensive; English-speaking countries, on the other hand, hold the opposite view. There are the usual data on cameras and other equipment.

The pictures themselves are divided into six sections: studio studies, female; outdoor studies, female; men; children; hands; and women in action. The first section is by far the biggest, taking up nearly half the 200 plates. Personally, however, I prefer the outdoor shots.

While the female models are nude, the men who are photographed are all wearing briefs or swimming costumes, and there are two men wrestling vigorously in each shot! Surely this is the first time we have seen that in a book. There are 12 pages of photographs of naked children, which would bring down instant wrath upon the photographer if published today. The 'women in action' section contains nothing more exciting than studio shots of various models dancing or lifting small objects.

Several of the models are the same as those used by Everard in previous books, and I suspect that some of the shots were taken at the same time as the earlier ones. Well, there's no harm in that.

✦ Pamela

Marks, Harrison,
Luxor Press, Size 9½" x 7¼"

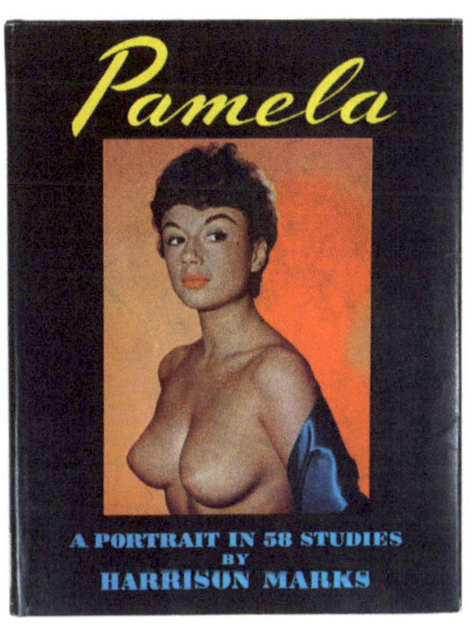

The dust jacket is in colour but the remainder of the book is in black and white. 'Pamela' was the late Pamela Green, who was perhaps the most famous nude model of the 1950s and '60s. Her only rivals were June Palmer and Lorraine Burnett. The photographer, George Harrison Marks, was arguably the successor to Roye, in that he came to the fore at about the time when Roye left England; and Marks too became something of a minor celebrity. At the time of writing, Pamela Green has a website (www.pamelagreen.com) dedicated to her memory; this provides, among other things, a mini-biography. Pamela had studied art at St Martin's School of Art, and she met Harrison Marks when she was performing in the *Folies Bergère* at the Prince of Wales Theatre in 1953. In those days Marks was a theatrical photographer, and the two of them formed a personal and professional partnership. In 1957 they began to publish the monthly magazine *Kamera*, which is probably the single most collected magazine of that period. The partnership was dissolved in 1967.

Given the title, it is not surprising that the book contains photographs of one model only, though Pamela makes such good use of wigs that a casual observer would probably think that several models had been used. There are three sections, entitled respectively: by the shore; studio nudes; and the art of glamour.

For my money, this is perhaps the most successful series of nudes offered by any photographer to date. Pamela Green had a perfect figure, classical in its proportions, and her theatrical experience gave her matchless poise. It is notable that, at this stage of her career, her hair was almost black, though in later years she was usually seen as a blonde. An outstanding model is, of course, a marvellous advantage for any photographer, but Marks had a complete mastery of technique.

Pamela's website reveals that, once *Kamera* became a success, the Marks studio was employing 15 people! And the constant pressure to produce new work led, inevitably, to a decline in standards. I suspect, in fact, that many of the 1960s magazine shots which were nominally taken by Marks were actually taken by an assistant while the boss was elsewhere.

All in all, this is a superb book. I have a copy signed by both model and photographer. It was bought for £8 in Oxford more than a decade ago, but you would be hard put to find a similar copy at that price today.

I seem to remember Pamela telling me that she and Marks never received any income for this book from the publisher, Luxor Press. That doesn't surprise me, given that Luxor press was run by Charles Skilton, a lecherous rogue. And it would account for Marks becoming his own publisher with his next book.

◆ In Camera

Everard, John,
Hale, Size 12½" x 10"

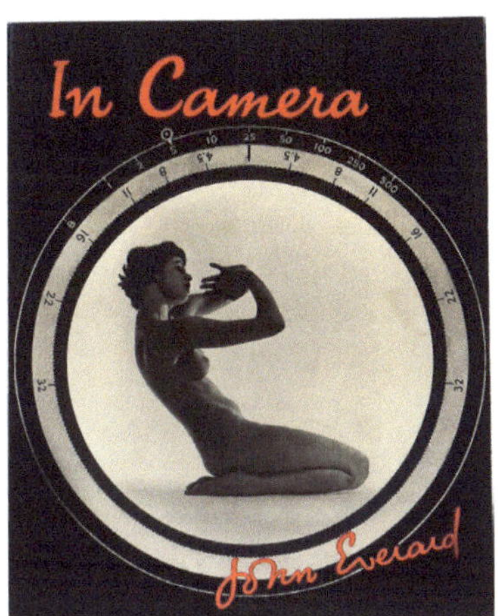

It's 1957, but we still can't quite bring ourselves to publish a book of nudes just for the hell of it. In the late 1950s no one could possibly say, 'Here are some fabulously beautiful women, photographed without any clothes on, and presented just for your enjoyment.' Well, they could say that, but they couldn't hope to remain respectable if they did, and they would very likely attract the attention of Inspector Knacker of the Yard.

So, this time John Everard's nudes come under the cover of a text which shares with the reader 'the technical methods and trade secrets' which lie behind his work. There is a foreword, followed by four chapters with the following titles: background to figure photography; studio and equipment; the finer points of studio technique; and creative photography.

These chapters occupy 36 quite large pages, and even today they are not without interest. For instance, Everard complains that 'while figure modelling is suffering from its present loss of prestige', girls are reluctant to pose for him. The sections on equipment and developers and so on are of course decades out of date, but they do shed light on the practices of the period. Everard's conclusion is that 'nude photography is one of the most exasperating, disappointing, elusive, yet finally rewarding and delightful occupations of man.'

We then have 31 plates, most of them a single study occupying the whole right-hand page. The left-hand page gives technical data and comments. These are all studio shots and without exception are very fine examples of Everard's work. He had not spent 25 years at the job without learning how to do it well.

◆ Figure Studies

Henle, Fritz,
Owen

Not seen, but reported to be 10" x 8". Henle was an American photographer, and the book was originally published in New York in 1954 by The Studio, in association with the Thomas V. Crowell Co. The 1954 edition is said to have been available in the UK, but in any event Peter Owen saw fit to publish a separate edition in 1957.

The book includes an introduction by one Jacquelyn Judge, and has 72 pages in all. There are 47 pages of black and white images, mostly outdoor nudes, with some photographic data. The book must have been a success, because it was reprinted in New York in 1962.

✦ Portfolio of Beauty

Kingswood, Tony, editor,
Photoart Publications, Size 10" x 7"

Interestingly, the inside flap of the dust jacket says that 'The book needs no justification', and the introduction maintains that the reader should 'enjoy this book with the same frank pleasure that the photographers experienced in creating the pictures for their own enjoyment'. These are courageous statements, and they constitute a pronounced improvement over the endless 'studies for artists' nonsense.

The title page declares that this is 'A collection of 60 examples of the best contemporary figure studies by the world's camera artists.' The principal English photographers represented are Stephen Glass (8 photographs) and Eva Grant (9). (Eva Grant was actually Greek by birth, but she had been living and working in England for many years.) Of the other 10 photographers, the Frenchmen Belorgé and Roland Carré are the best known.

The publisher who issued this book also produced the magazine *Photoart*, which appeared monthly for about four years from September 1955. The book was probably sold mainly by mail order, through that magazine. It is divided into sections, such as 'Patterns and moods in the artist's studio' and 'Studies taken in the Great Outdoors'. It is tolerably well printed, on heavy paper. The pictures appear on the right-hand pages only, the left page carrying notes by the editor; few of these notes tell us anything which we could not work out for ourselves.

All in all, a pleasant book, containing images by quite a number of well-known photographers who never had a book devoted solely to their own work.

1958

✦ Nude Pattern

de Dienes, André,
John Lane, Size 11" x 9"

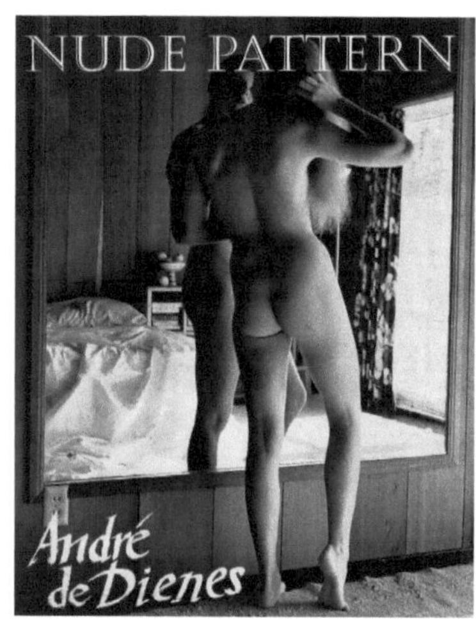

There is a foreword by Norman Hall, editor of *Photography*. While short, it contains much good sense. He speaks of the 'essential eroticism of the naked body' and the 'Victorian fear of the body'. He recognises de Dienes's craftsmanship, but attributes his success, rightly I think, to his ability to make his models feel completely at ease.

The images themselves (105 in all) are really quite stunning. André de Dienes had by this time been living in Hollywood for some years, and he took full advantage of the availability of voluptuous models and plentiful sunshine. His original photographic prints were evidently exposed in a way which avoided the burnt-out highlights which so bedevil much nude photography, and the printing of this book does full justice to the original negatives;

the skin tones are marvellous. All in all, this book can lay claim to being the most impressive collection of nudes published in England up to this time. The fact that it was the work of a man who was born in Transylvania and was then working in Hollywood tells us much, I think, about the stultifying effect of decades of English prudery.

✦ Kamera on Location

Marks, Harrison,
Kamera Publications, Size 10" x 8¼"

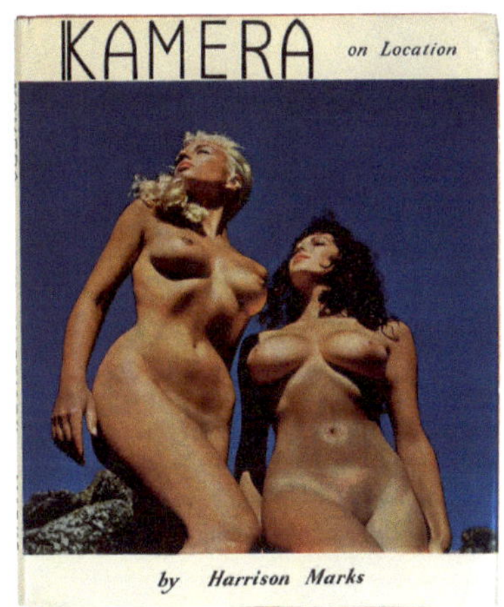

The dust jacket is a stunner: it carries a full-colour picture of a nude Pamela Green, together with another model. The shot is taken from about knee height, looking up, with a deep-blue sky as background; it was presumably taken with a polaroid filter, and the girls have fabulous skin tones. On the back of the jacket are four black and white shots.

Marks seems to have followed Roye into profitable self-publishing, because this book is published by 'Kamera Publications', and *Kamera* was, of course, the title of his famous monthly magazine.

The very first shot in the book is a reproduction of the dust-jacket image, which is just as well because probably few of the original dust jackets survive at this distance in time. There then follows a foreword by the author/photographer. This reveals that the 82 pages of black and white photographs which the book contains were all shot on a remote Scottish island in the Hebrides. Or so Marks said. Pamela Green told me, in 2008, that actually the location was in the Scilly Isles, but Marks wanted to keep the place a secret. In any event, Marks gives some account of the practical difficulties involved in conducting a lengthy shoot in such a remote site. When the photographer and his models eventually returned to London, they had 1,000 monochrome and 400 colour images to choose from.

It seems to me that there are only three models used here in total, but the clever use of wigs, and the variety of poses adopted, make it look as if there are more. Pamela Green is heavily featured, of course; the second model is Lorraine Burnett, and the third is Marie Deveraux. In my view, Marks at his best was the only English photographer to rival André de Dienes in capturing the eroticism and sexuality of his models. Judging by the snippets of biographical and autobiographical material which I have read over the years, Marks was a fairly promiscuous man, uninhibited about sexual matters. This is reflected in his work. To put it crudely, these women look as if they know what it's for – and it's not for stirring the tea. There is a final page listing the technical data for each shot: aperture, speed, filter, and so on. As usual, this information should be taken with a pinch of salt.

On the day when I wrote this description, I searched the internet for a secondhand copy of this book. I found one: at £220. But you can get it cheaper in Germany.

◆ **Unique Editions Nos. 1, 2, 3, and 4**

Roye,

Art Publications, Size 8¼" x 6¼"

Art Publications was, of course, one of Roye's own companies. As you have been reminded more than once, this is a bibliography of hardback books, and the first thing to be said about these four publications is that they are not hardbacks; indeed they are barely even books. Each of the *Unique Editions* is a card-bound set of four pictures of female nudes, the inside cover being marked 'A limited edition for private circulation'.

The images are nearly all ones which appeared earlier, in one or other of Roye's various books, and the model most frequently seen in Desirée, who had a Roye book all to herself in 1942. But here there is one vital difference. In these four booklets the photographs are reproduced entirely unretouched. In other words, if I may labour the point, the models' pubic hair is clearly visible. No attempt whatever has been made to disguise it.

Roye clearly knew that in publishing photographs in this form – even for 'private circulation' – he was testing the law. The first booklet carries a brief foreword, and in it he mentions the famous 1954 decision of Swindon magistrates to order the destruction of copies of Boccaccio's *Decameron* – a work of literature which had been famous for 600 years. In describing the magistrates' decision as absurd, Roye was almost daring the authorities to take action against him. Well, take action they did.

In May and June of 1958 Roye was twice prosecuted for publishing an 'obscene libel'; that is to say, he was prosecuted for nothing more elaborate than publishing a picture of a nude model with her pubic hair showing. The outcome of this trial will be discussed under the year 1960, when Roye published an account of his prosecution with the title *Unique Verdict*. For the moment, however, let us just note that these modest booklets, and their treatment by the authorities, constitute a turning-point in English social history. From here on, it would prove almost impossible for the police and the Home Office to hold the line against publishing nudes 'as nature made them'.

In fact, of course, the whole case was utterly ridiculous. This can be testified by any man who was an adult at around the end of the 1950s. Although prudery was still widespread in England at that stage, it was also true that any adult could wander into a Soho bookshop and, in a small room at the back, buy hardcore photographs showing erections, penetration, bondage, fellatio, and anything else that took your fancy. I myself bought such pictures at about that time. And if I, a callow youth from the provinces, could discover such things, then the availability of real porn must have been blindingly obvious to every adult male in London.

We also know that, certainly by the 1970s, the Obscene Publications Squad was thoroughly corrupt. (For details, see *The Fall of Scotland Yard* by Barry Cox.) A judge who jailed 12 members of Scotland Yard's 'dirty squad' in the 1970s said that they were involved in an 'evil conspiracy which turned the Obscene Publications Act into a vast protection racket'. In other words, if a Soho porn broker paid up, he could sell whatever he pleased. 'We bought our own justice,' said one operator. 'And the more we paid, the better justice we got.' David McGillivray, an expert on censorship and sex, has remarked that in the 1970s the Soho porn business was run by vicious thugs. And those were just the police.

Roye, unfortunately, is no longer with us, and we cannot ask him exactly what happened. But I suspect that, in the early part of 1958, he may have been offered an opportunity to buy immunity from prosecution, and that he told the police officers precisely where they could stuff it. He was a very proud and determined man, and was not likely to succumb to corrupt pressure of that kind.

◆ Nudes of Jean Straker

Straker, Jean,
Skilton, Size 11" x 8¾"

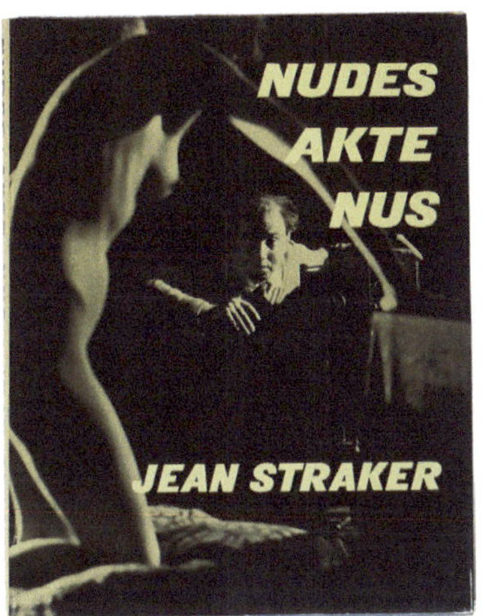

'Jean' Straker, incidentally, was a man. And the book contains nudes by him rather than of him. This book was also published by Charles Skilton, who was the man behind the Luxor Press, among other imprints. Luxor was a firm which published such titles as *Lesbian Secrets* and *The School for Sin*. Let's hope that Straker had better luck with royalties than Harrison Marks did.

I have no idea how many copies of this book were printed, but the text comes in three languages, English, German, and French, so Skilton evidently tried to cover his printing costs with sales in Europe as well as the UK. My copy declares that it is one of a special edition, bound in leather, and is no. 98 of a total of 110, signed by the author/photographer.

The book is divided into seven sections, each devoted to a particular approach to photography as practised at Straker's lecture-demonstrations. The sections are: Femina projects (slightly surrealistic images with nudes); figure studies (fairly orthodox); lighting effects; essays in composition; classical studies; Group Omega (in lighter vein); and pinups.

Straker had premises in Soho Square, London, where he seems to have run courses in photography. According to his own foreword, these courses made frequent reference to painting, including study of the work of Rembrandt, Titian, and Tintoretto.

There are 61 photographic plates in all, and they are more than usually interesting. Straker made made heavy use of props, and introduced mysterious figures in the background (usually male). Enigmatic is perhaps the best description of some of his work.

Straker's models are mostly excellent, and include some faces and figures which are familiar from the work of Roye and Everard. Plate XXIV, unless my eyes deceive me, shows an extremely young Lorraine Burnett, and must have been taken before her famous bust was fully developed. Another of his models, also very young, is one I remember seeing in some hardcore shots from the 1950s. All in all, this is an interesting selection of this photographer's work, and it is the only book he ever published.

To go back to the foreword for a moment… 'It is right,' says Straker, 'that society shall protect itself against a degrading exploitation of the baser instincts; but it is equally important that its intellect shall remain unshackled.' What Straker is saying here, in a form of code, is that it is ridiculous to have to avoid showing pubic hair.

In the late 1950s and early 1960s I used to read a glossy and well-printed magazine called *The Studio*, which covered the world of art. Somewhere around 1960 – I cannot give a precise date – I noticed that, in the back of this magazine, Straker began to advertise photographs of nudes for sale. And he did so, interestingly enough, by printing a striking sample of his work showing a female nude with a very clear and totally unmistakable patch of black pubic hair.

Adverts for nude photographs were, of course, frequently seen in men's magazines, but an unretouched image was most unusual – in fact, probably unique. Most sellers of such material preferred not to end up in Wormwood Scrubs.

I well remember, at about this time, sitting in the reference room of my local library when a young man came in, picked *The Studio* off the shelf, and sat down to read it. I assumed that he would immediately turn to Straker's advert in the back; but no, he seemed to be genuinely interested in art, because he read through the magazine slowly. I kept an eye on him, because I wanted to see what his reaction was when he reached the Straker page. And, as I expected, he practically jumped out of his chair with shock. After a moment or two's contemplation of what was then a truly startling image, he came over to me and asked if he could borrow my pen. 'You don't often see an address like that,' he commented, but I was too tactful to ask him what address he was going to copy down.

The editors of *The Studio*, like Straker, must have known exactly what risks they were taking, and must have calculated either that they would not be prosecuted, or that, if they were, they could put forward the defence that the picture was artistic rather than pornographic.

Straker does in fact seem to have been prosecuted. In researching this book, I found an internet reference which said that Straker's nude studies 'became the subject of the photographic equivalent of the Lady Chatterley obscenity trial in the 1960s.' In other words, as suggested above, Straker's defence was that he was an artist, not a porn merchant. What the outcome of the case actually was, I do not know, but whether the prosecuting authorities won or lost in that particular instance does not much matter at this distance in time. The fact is, every time a prosecution of that kind was brought, it left the law looking ever more absurd and ridiculous.

✦ The Female Form.

Various (but evidently edited by Fritz Henle),

Arco

Not seen. Size reportedly 10" x 7". This book was originally published in the US in 1957, by Milestone Books, with the title *Photography Interpretations*. Interestingly, the Library of Congress catalogue has no trace of such a book. A search of the British Library catalogue, under the UK title, also draws a blank.

Fritz Henle provides an introduction, after which the book consists of a series of written and photographic essays on the female form:

  I: An essay on the head by Walter Sarff.

 II: An essay on the breast by Peter Basch.

III: An essay on the hand by Roger Prigent.

IV: An essay on the torso by André de Dienes.

 V: An essay on the leg by Alan Fontaine.

VI: An essay on the back by Philip O. Stearns.

There are about 130 pages of photographs, with one colour plate. Judging by the price demanded for secondhand copies, this book is evidently much sought-after by US collectors.

1959

✦ Model in Movement

Everard, John,

The Bodley Head, Size 11" x 8½"

John Everard published his first book of nudes in 1935, and here he is again, still at it. (His last book, *Model in Shadow*, would appear in 1965, after the closing date of this bibliography.) By this time, Everard seems to have been living in South Africa, and this book has a preface by Professor R. Bain, head of the art school in Johannesburg. Bain makes the point that the title of the book is significant: these shots are nearly all of models whose movement has been frozen in time by a fast shutter speed.

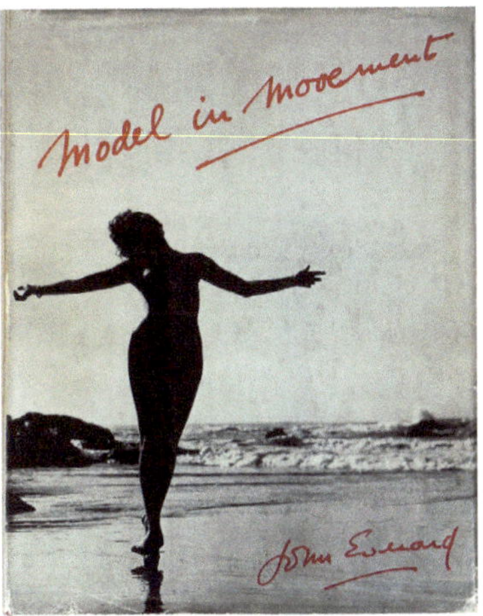

There follows an introduction by Everard himself, who tells us, not for the first time, that after each book he tends to conclude that he has done all that can be done with the nude, only to find, on reflection, that there are other avenues to explore. This introduction is still of considerable interest to anyone who is thinking of photographing nudes. The book is divided into four parts: I, women in the studio; II, women out of doors; III, women in 'intermittent action'; and IV, women and men in 'continuous action sequences'. Each of these sections has a brief introduction of its own.

The studio shots are fairly orthodox in lighting and in the way the models are posed, but some of them differ from Everard's previous work in that the models have been captured, as the book's title promises, while in movement, chiefly dancing; and in one case fencing. This makes for some attractive images, though the retouching is blindingly obvious, and irritating, in some cases.

The outdoor shots, many taken beside the sea, are particularly successful, though on one page, I note, Everard pokes gentle fun at his colleague Roye's shot entitled 'Bank Holiday at Brighton' – in *Eves without Leaves* (1940). Quite a few of the shots include more than one model, and there are a great many images overall – sometimes as many as eight to the page.

The 'intermittent action' section is shot in the studio and on what looks like a garden patio, and is less interesting. The pages featuring a nude ballet dancer on points are something not often seen before, though Eva Grant took some similar images which appeared in her monthly magazine *Line and Form*.

Finally the 'continuous action' shots are, as the description suggests, rapid-sequence photographs of a model skipping, jumping, and so forth, rather in the Eadweard Muybridge tradition. They were taken with a special camera which exposed six frames a second, but even so they presented considerable technical difficulties. On the whole I feel that the results do not justify the trouble involved, though for once they might be of genuine value to artists. Incidentally, the nude men and women in this last section do not appear together, and the men are clothed in jockstraps and leopard-skin underwear.

Overall this is an excellent collection, and one which an enthusiast for this form of photography would be well advised to search for on the secondhand market.

1960

✦ Young Nudes

Nakamura, Masaya,
Paterson

Not seen. Reported to be 12" x 9¾". According to the British Library catalogue, this book was published in Tokyo in 1960 by CamerArt Publications, and was edited by one Koen Shigemori. Presumably it was simply imported into the UK by Paterson.

There is a five-page introduction with some technical data, and the book contains 71 black and white photogravure plates featuring Oriental models. A modern bookseller states that the photographs are all artistic poses; they are not explicit, and indeed are tame by today's standards.

✦ Unique Verdict – the Story of an Unsuccessful Prosecution

Roye,

Art Publications, Size 5¼" x 4¼"

A booklet with a card cover. This is the booklet that I referred to when describing Roye's 1958 publications, *Unique Editions* Nos. 1 to 4. You will have noted, perhaps, that no hardback books containing nude photographs were published in England in 1959, and only one imported book was issued in 1960. The reason for that is surely obvious: publishers just didn't know where they stood in relation to the law.

Unique Verdict includes a short account of Roye's brush with the authorities. He relates how, shortly after issuing the four *Unique Editions,* he was charged with 'publishing an obscene libel'. This meant that his crime lay in selling a series of photographs in which the pubic hair of his models was clearly visible. (Incidentally, the *Unique Editions* were not for sale to the general public; they were available only to subscribers to the Camera Studies Club.)

In May and June 1958, Roye was subjected to two trials at the London sessions. At the first of these, 10 of the 12 jurors wished to stop the trial as soon as they had heard Roye give evidence. At that time, however, if a jury could not reach a unanimous verdict a retrial had to be held. At the second trial Roye was acquitted.

It is quite clear from this booklet that a considerable volume of evidence was put forward by the defence to demonstrate that Roye was a man with an impeccable record and that he had international standing as a photographer of outstanding ability. One of the points mentioned was that, duirng the Second World War, he had been invited to assist the Political Intelligence Department of the Foreign Office. It is also quite clear that his defending counsel argued that he was an 'artist' and not some run-of-the-mill vulgarian.

While in the witness box, Roye was asked why he had published *Unique Editions.* He replied that he shared the view held by most serious workers in the difficult field of photography that to remove hair by retouching was to sacrifice one's artistic integrity. He had decided, he said, that the time was appropriate to publish a book free of mutilation by retouching. He had a feeling of satisfaction that he was once again breaking new ground in his profession.

All of which is clear enough. In the remaining pages of the booklet, Roye reproduces the eight photographs (still, of course, totally unretouched) which had made up *Unique Editions* Nos 1 and 2, together with some of the letters of support which he had received from all over the world.

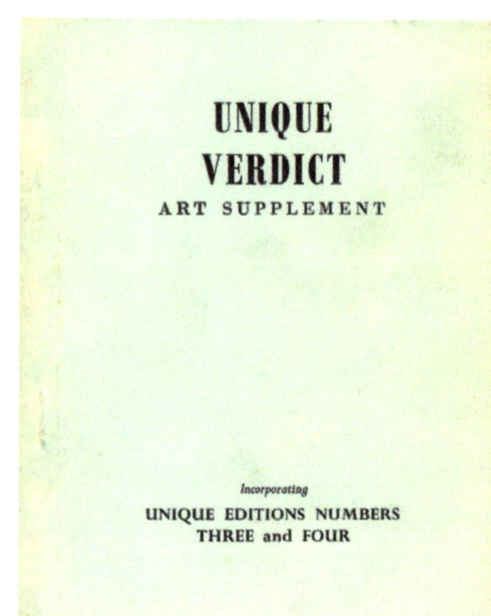

✦ Unique Verdict – Art Supplement

Roye,
Art Publications

Not seen, but beyond doubt a card-covered booklet, size 5¼" x 4¼", that is a companion to *Unique Verdict*.

This booklet included the eight pictures from *Unique Editions* Nos. 3 and 4, which, as mentioned in the previous entry, could now be published complete with the models' pubic hair without fear of a further visit from Inspector Knacker of the Yard.

Why, you may ask, didn't Roye include all 16 of the original photographs in the one volume? Because he never wasted an opportunity to make money, that's why! Why give the punter everything for one payment when you can easily persuade him to pay twice?

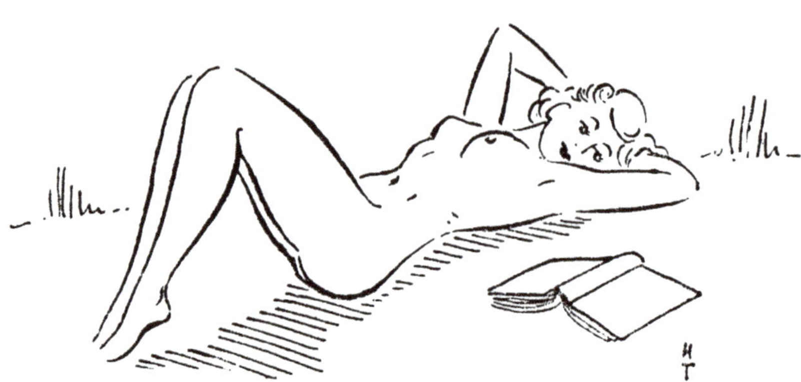

ENVOI

ROYE'S ACCOUNT OF the failed prosecution against him constitutes a good point, I think, to bring this bibliography to a close. For we are now at the start of the 1960s, a decade in which almost everything would change.

It has been said that Freud made sex intellectually respectable in the 1930s, and that Kinsey made it socially respectable in the 1950s. Well, respectable or not, the 1960s would see a lot more of sex in all its various forms. Let us take a few examples from the entertainment industry, in order to see how rapidly a more liberal attitude towards sexual matters emerged.

Nudity had been banned in films in the UK for decades. However, in the 1950s, British and French films about nudism began to be shown. These early nudie pics lacked 'full frontals', but in 1968 the Scandinavian film *Hugs and Kisses* was presented to the UK film censor with an actress's pubic hair clearly visible. The censor asked for the scene to be cut, and this request did not pass without comment. The press generally considered that the censor's attitude was ridiculous, and within a few months pubic hair was on show in several films.

In 1963 a live girl appeared nude at a 'happening' at the Edinburgh Festival, causing a huge scandal among the prudish Scots. But by 1967 full-frontal male nudes were on show (albeit briefly, and in shadow) in the West End musical *Hair*. In 1968 theatre censorship was abolished in the UK. And in 1969 *Oh Calcutta* opened in New York; this was a show which featured both male and female nudes, moving freely on stage with very little modesty indeed, and it soon transferred to London.

In the world of book publishing, 1960 was when the authorities brought their famous case against Penguin for publishing D.H. Lawrence's *Lady Chatterley's Lover*. This novel had been famous since the 1930s but no publisher had previously dared to issue it because it featured graphic descriptions of sexual intercourse, complete with the traditional four-letter words for the sexual organs and sexual acts. When Penguin virtually invited the authorities to prosecute them for obscenity if they dared, the challenge was taken up.

The prosecution proved to be totally inept. The prosecuting counsel, Mervyn Griffith-Jones, was stupid enough to ask the jury: 'Would you want your wife or servants to read this book?' This inevitably reinforced the idea that the judiciary was out of touch with ordinary people, and the jury acquitted the publishers of any offence. Within a year, two million copies of the book had been sold (far more than it deserved, in my opinion).

And so on.

All of these loosenings of what had previously been tightly laced corsets led to *Time* magazine's famous article of 1966, in which the UK's capital city was renamed as 'Swinging London'.

What happened in society at large was reflected in photography. Roye and Jean Straker had led the way, and others cautiously followed. Because so many publishers of books and magazines had been prosecuted in the past, there was no immediate rush; but, by the end of the 1960s, images which would have been unthinkable only a few years earlier were now so commonplace as to cause hardly the raising of an eyebrow.

In time, of course, many of those who had argued for a more liberal approach in the visual and literary arts came to be appalled at some of the stuff which was published once it was clear that prosecution was unlikely to follow. But that is the nature of freedom, I'm afraid. If you, the famous and dedicated artist, have the freedom to maintain your own 'artistic integrity', however you see fit, then others can exercise that freedom too, as they see fit. And if they choose to use your hard-earned freedom to make money in a crude and tasteless fashion, then that's just your hard luck.

In short, soon after 1960, the classical era of English nude photography came to an end. We would soon enter the world of full-frontal, gynaecological nudes in full colour.

This bibliography will serve as a reminder of the more restrained times and the more prudish customs and practices which prevailed between the invention of photography and 1960; and it provides a record of the photographers of the nude who published their work in book form. Their output now seems not only classical but, in many instances, rather quaint. In their day, however, they were brave pioneers, fully deserving of our respect.

That's the end of this modest little book. If you feel inclined to buy any of the volumes referred to herein, a great place to start is on the database of many thousands of secondhand book dealers, known as Abebooks. If you live in the UK, go to abebooks.co.uk, and in the US it's abebooks.com. Good hunting.

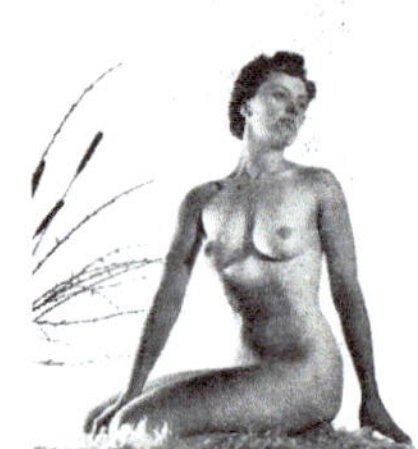

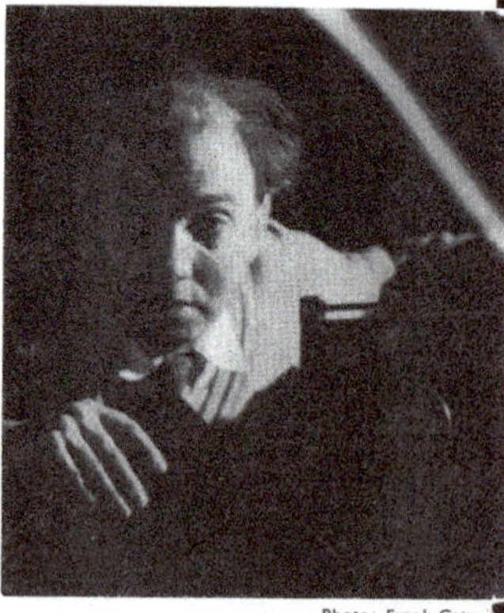

Index

This index lists only those photographers and others whose name is listed in the bibliography as the 'author' of a particular book. The titles of that author's books are then listed in order of publication. Finally, of course, the page number for each entry is given. The index does not include occasional mentions of photographers' names which occur within the body of the text.

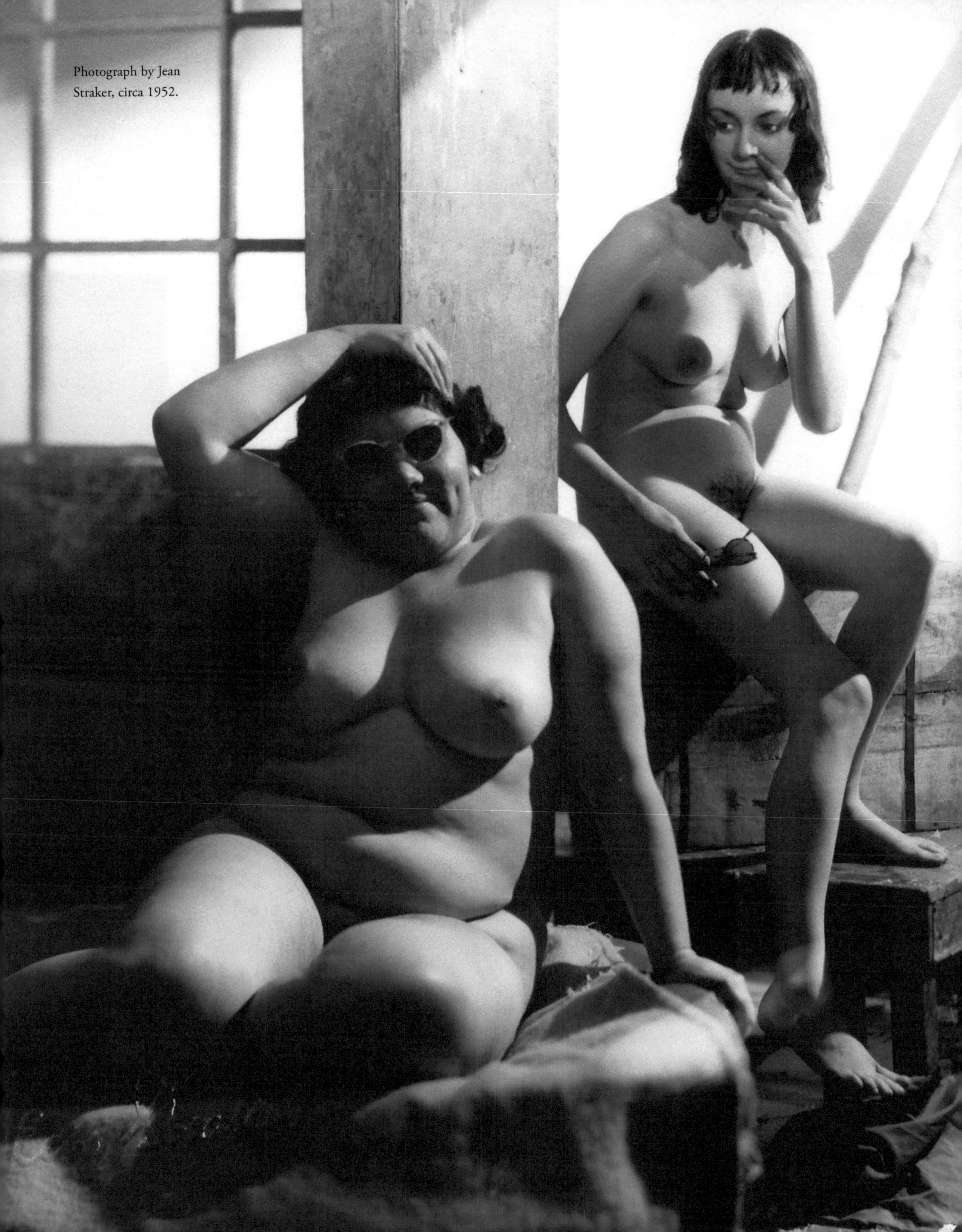

Photograph by Jean
Straker, circa 1952.

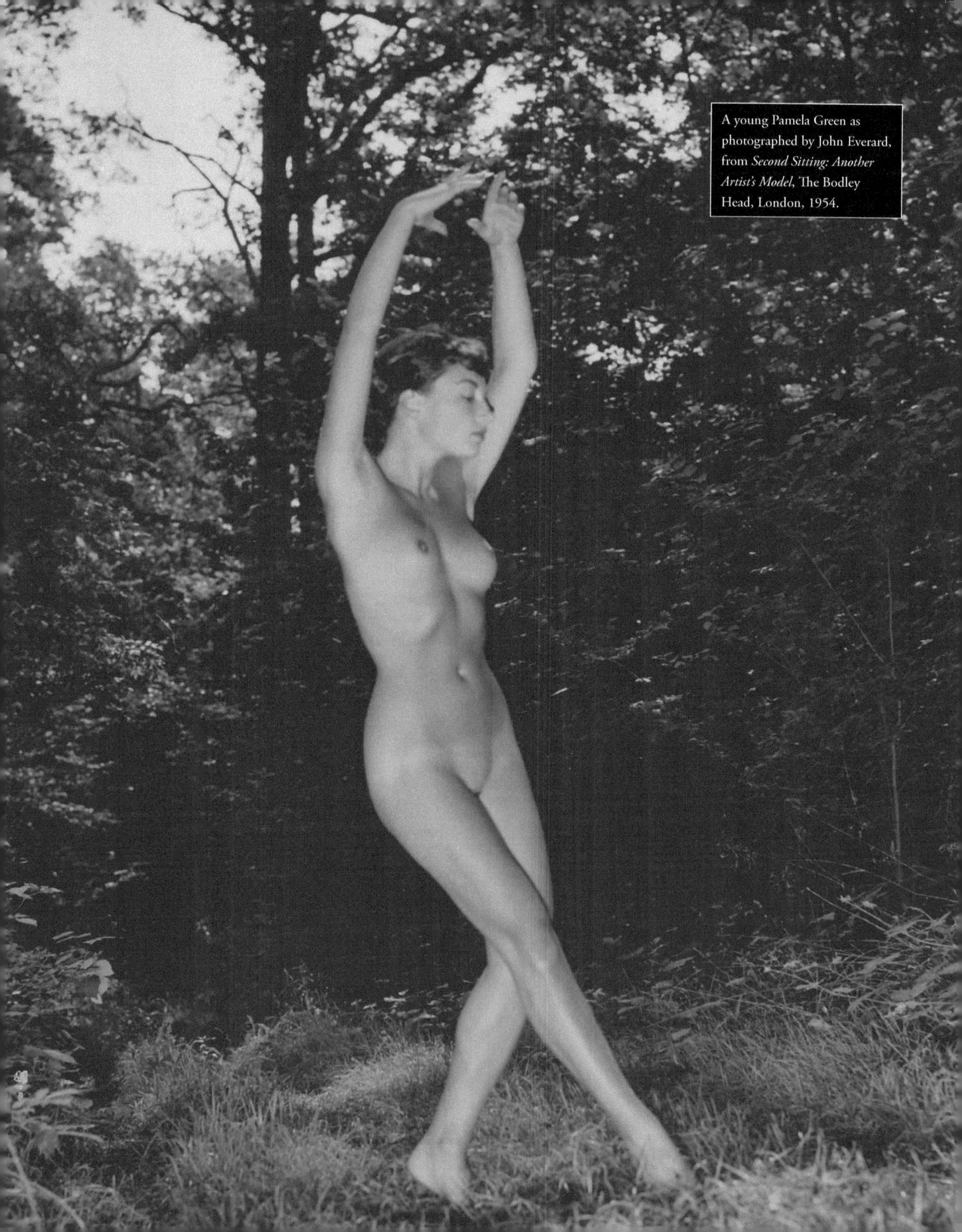

A young Pamela Green as photographed by John Everard, from *Second Sitting: Another Artist's Model*, The Bodley Head, London, 1954.

AVAILABLE TITLES FROM WOLFBAIT

Doing Rude Things

The history of the British sex film.

NEW! **Cinema au Naturel**

A history of nudist film.

Miniten: Rules of the Game

Invented in the 1930s, Miniten is a
tennis-like game played by naturists.

Naked as Nature Intended

The epic tale of a nudist picture by Pamela Green,
with photographs by Douglas "Dambuster" Webb, DFM.

The Naked Truth About Harrison Marks

The notorious biography by Franklyn Wood.

Past Masters of the Nude

An illustrated bibliography of nude photography
books published in England from 1896 to 1960.

THE STEPHEN GLASS COLLECTION

Amazons of Yesteryear

A rare, action-packed collection of images of
wrestling women of the 1940s and 1950s.

Beauty Off-Duty

Relaxed, everyday moments caught on camera.

Naked in the Menagerie

A playful look at Eve accompanied by her animal friends.

Nudist Camp Follies – volumes 1 and 2

An intimate look at the natural
and free atmosphere in Sun Clubs.

Nymphs and Naiads

Beauty unadorned and outdoors.

NEW! **Poise and Pose**

A magnificent series of photographs
of female beauty taken in the studio.

Order online at wolfbait.co.uk

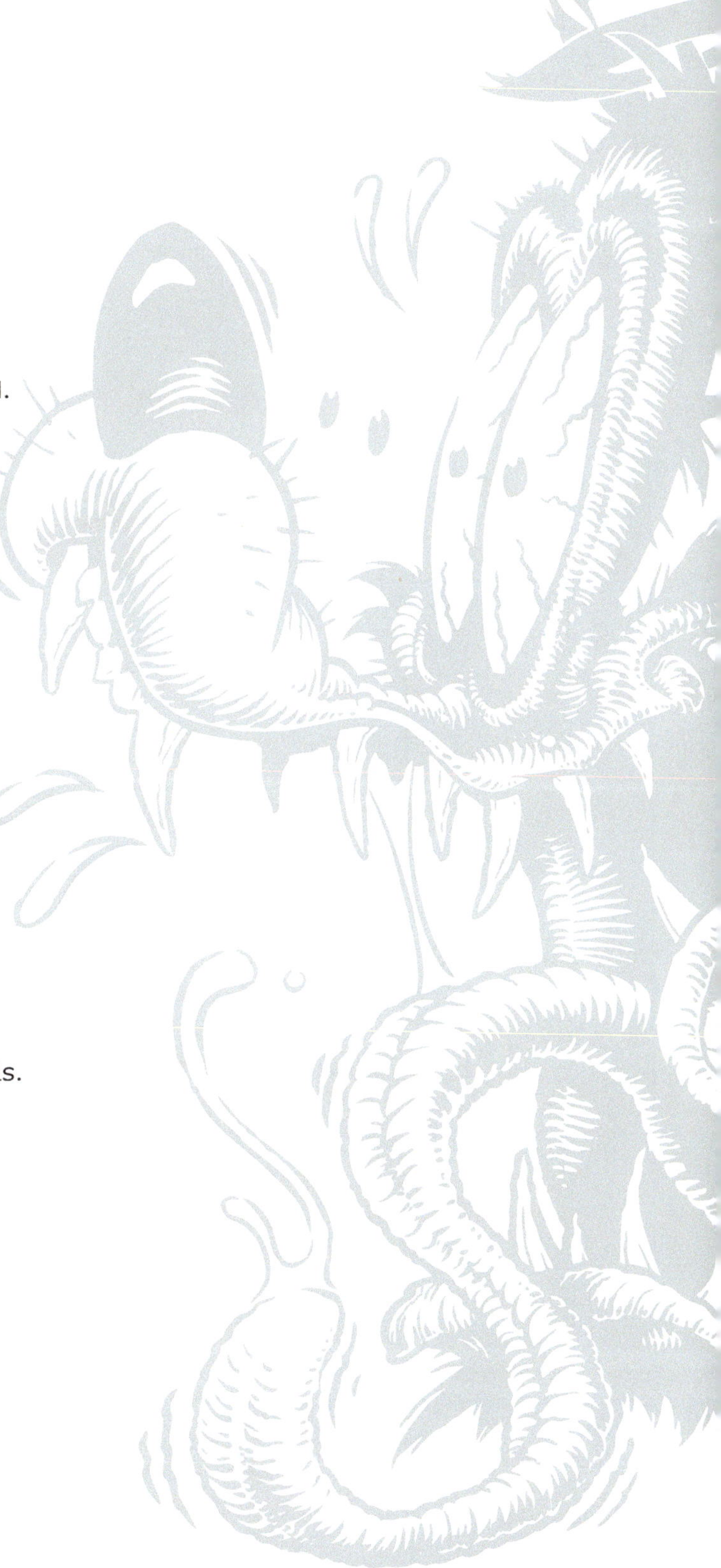

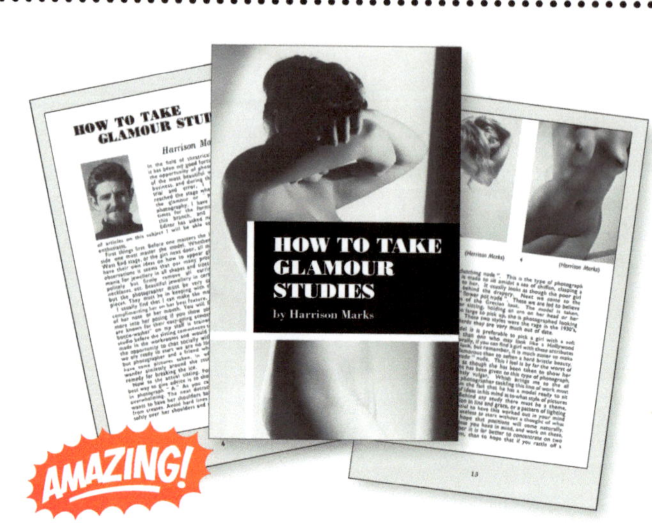
HOW TO TAKE GLAMOUR STUDIES
by Harrison Marks
AMAZING!

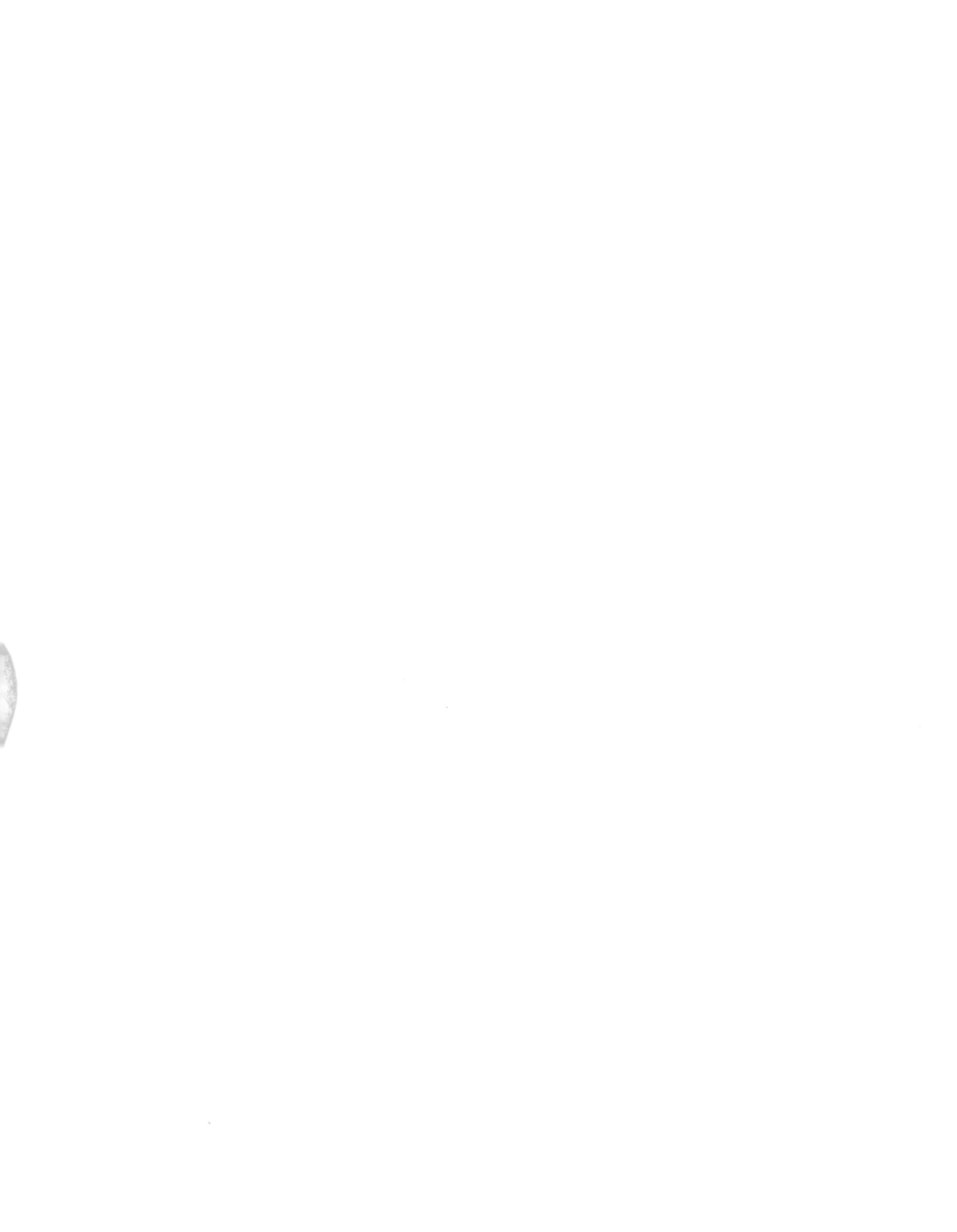